"I launched my startup while in college and juggled school, personal relationships and my startup. It was no easy task. I wish *The College Student Startup Guide* would have been there to guide me through the chaos."

— Henry Schwartz, Founder, Mobcraft Beer
and Shark Tank Contestant

"Being in college while you have a startup is no easy task. Having gone through it, I always had Gee to help keep me on the track to succeed. The lessons in his new book, *The College Student Startup Guide* are invaluable not only for your startup, but also for your personal growth."

— Jake Smith, Manager of Operations at Bird

"Coming up with a startup idea is easy. Successfully executing that idea into a thriving startup is a completely different story. Gee's new book, *The College Student Startup Guide*, helps provide student entrepreneurs the critical insights needed to go from idea to launch."

— Chris Roche, Founder, Recruit Chute

"You could get several college degrees to get all of these insights, or you could just buy Gee's book. The choice is yours."

— Jocelyn Kopac, Founder, The Digital Market

"Launching a startup while you are in college can change your life. *The College Student Startup Guide* shows you how."

— Ben Morales, Founder, Latino Pro

D1125157

"Gee's book takes the guesswork out of how to build a great startup while in college. He has gathered what no college student get could in any one classroom. He provides insights through interviewing world-class angel investors, venture capitalists, intellectual property attorneys and, of course, college student startup founders."

— Jeff Peterson, Founder, Geneva Supply

"When I started building my first startup, I quickly learned that you need to understand, finance, marketing, law, software development and more. No college major provides you all that information, *The College Student Startup Guide* does."

— Kristen Holtan, Co-Founder, Blue Line Battery

"*The College Student Startup Guide* not only provides actionable insights, it also gives readers a step-by-step process to follow to ensure the greatest probability of startup success."

— Austin Beveridge, Marketing Manager, Bolt

"Make no mistake. This is not a textbook. *The College Student Startup Guide* is a real world, hard hitting, step-by-step guide…practical, helpful, insightful, no-nonsense and sometimes funny. If you are launching a startup in college, this is a must have tool for you!"

— Anna Tracy, Founder, Greet Feet

THE COLLEGE STUDENT STARTUP GUIDE

12 Steps To Launch a Successful Startup

Dave Gee

Front cover features some of Gee's previous college-student entrepreneurs: From right to left: Ben Morales, Founder of Latino Pro | Anna Tracy, Founder of Greet Feet | Kristen Holtan, Co-Founder of Blue Line Battery | Jocelyn Kopac, Founder of The Digital Market | Ben Breitenbucher, Co-Founder of Blue Line Battery.

Copyediting by Michael Spanjar & Alex Aulisi
Cover design by Kristen Holtan
Graphic design by Anna Tracy
Cover photo by Nicole Holtan

Printed in the United States of America | First printing October 2019

Book available in a digital edition and print-on-demand.

ISBN: 9781687530752

10-19 – Second Edition

How Can This Book Help You?

College students today have more opportunities and more demands on their time than any point in history. The stress of going to classes, studying for exams, having personal relationships and sometimes holding down a job can feel overwhelming. Now, imagine trying to launch a successful startup while juggling all those responsibilities. It may seem impossible but it's not if you have a well-executed plan.

Building a solid plan means implementing the proven, critical steps that have helped college students land multi-million-dollar contracts, pitch their businesses on Shark Tank, raise millions in startup capital, and continue to grow their exciting organizations.

Of course, not all startup ideas become rapidly-growing businesses. Some of the students who achieved these successes also struggled to balance relationships, some had their GPAs spiral out of control and yes, some even contemplated dropping out of college. I interviewed these students so I could share their hard-hitting, real-world insights.

The students I have helped with their startups don't even always launch their businesses. There are many others who launch their startups but don't continue the businesses after graduation. However, even the ones who don't launch a successful startup learn skills beyond anything that can be learned in a classroom. These students have applied these lessons at some of the fastest growing startups in the world.

This year I was reflecting on these students' experiences and realized that I needed to share their stories with other college students who might be considering launching their own startup. But I wanted to go further, so I added interviews that I personally conducted with world-class angel investors, venture capitalists, researchers, intellectual property attorneys and, of course, entrepreneurs.

The end result I have created for you is *The College Student Startup Guide. This book is insightful, practical, powerful, sometimes funny and can help you get ready to fulfill your entrepreneurial dreams!*

—Gee

Table of Contents

My Personal Startup Journey...
Past, Present and Future

Speaking to you personally, I can tell you I have never experienced such professionally exhilarating moments (I am talking cranking AC/DC's *Back in Black* or Queen's *We are the Champions* in my car) as I did in each of my startups. Launching Sales Sherpas and making the first sale, securing an angel investment of $500,000 in Bungee, signing our partner contract with Salesforce, and making the first sale with Classmunity each got my adrenaline pumping. I then moved on to teaching marketing in the MBA program at the University of Wisconsin-Madison and now am directing the Launch Pad startup accelerator, teaching entrepreneurship and mentoring student entrepreneurs at the University of Wisconsin-Whitewater.

When it came to my startups, I found my satisfaction wasn't derived from earning the money itself, whether it be from sales or securing an investment in my startup, but from knowing I was helping people and companies. It was satisfying to know I was helping a small telecom company with a marketing plan, so they could compete with a large cable company. Another time I worked with my business partner to provide loyalty software to a company so the business could stay in the family. The school fundraising software company helped a school district buy a washing machine because the children didn't have a washing machine at home.

If you are thinking about launching your startup for the money, then you are in for a rude awakening. Forget the Lamborghinis, the private jets and millions in disposable income. Those could be a by-product, but the odds are long. Frankly, being an entrepreneur is a long and tough slog. Plan on months or longer without a paycheck (I once went six months with no paycheck and many sleepless nights), long hours, less time for boyfriends and girlfriends, pressure on personal relationships and a litany of other stressors. Think deeply about what is motivating you to launch this startup and stay laser focused on that throughout your entrepreneurial journey.

Over time, I have found myself consciously identifying a core personal motivating force, of helping people, and companies succeed... With Sales Sherpas, the primary motivator was simply to launch my first startup and frankly, to provide for my family after I lost my job.

With Bungee, I wanted to launch a software company and, obviously, continue to provide for my family. I decided at that point to shift my career to educating others about entrepreneurship, but also to continue some involvement with a startup.

With Classmunity, my co-founders and I wanted to help schools, and I personally wanted to make a conscious effort to create a startup with a female CEO.

My latest venture, is a personal one, I am now working on a startup idea, to help improve and save the lives of young adults.

Lastly, I truly love working with college students to help them fulfill their entrepreneurial dreams.

If you want to discover free cutting-edge insights into the startup world, the latest college student startup successes and my new startups and projects feel free to follow me on LinkedIn. linkedin.com/in/davidrgee/

Gee

Most Effective Use of this Guide

This guide was created with topics in the recommended chronological order from the time a college student has a startup idea all the way to managing a successful startup launch.

This is not a textbook that you use to cram for an exam. It is not a book to put next to your bed to fall asleep. *The College Student Startup Guide* is a roadmap to help you launch your startup. I recommend that you read a section, apply the information, then come back to the book to move on to the subsequent section.

Even if you major in a specific area (for example, if you are a marketing major), at least skim the section. You will find that despite your expertise, your plans will need to shift to adapt to the startup world, and that there is content in here you won't learn in the classroom. You might have to shift from the mindset of having an unlimited marketing budget in your classes to a marketing budget of $0; that's what happened to me. You have to get very creative and focused, in a hurry, in order to make your startup survive and thrive.

The Startup Readiness Assessment™, located in the appendix, will help you determine how truly ready you are to begin your entrepreneurial journey. When you have read the guide and implemented the steps, take the assessment to see if you are really prepared for your startup journey.

To quickly familiarize yourself with critical startup terminology, for every entrepreneur, review the section, "Terminology every entrepreneur must understand," located in the appendix.

The Startup World Today

Before we dive into the steps to help you, let's discuss the environment in which you will operate. Specifically, let's discover the trends in startup growth, or lack thereof, and secondarily, the sectors that have experienced the fastest growth. These insights can help you select a market is growing and which ones are dying.

First, let's look at Kauffman Foundation data to gain an understanding of the trends in startup activity. "The Rate of New Entrepreneurs" captures the percentage of the adult, non-business-owner population that started a business each month. This component was formerly known as the Kauffman Index of Entrepreneurial Activity and was presented in a series of reports over roughly a decade. The Rate of New Entrepreneurs, as measured here, captures all new business owners, including those who own incorporated or unincorporated businesses and those who are employers or non-employers. The Rate of New Entrepreneurs is calculated from matched data from the Current Population Survey (CPS). (Fairlie 2016).

2016 Kauffman Index Activity State Report

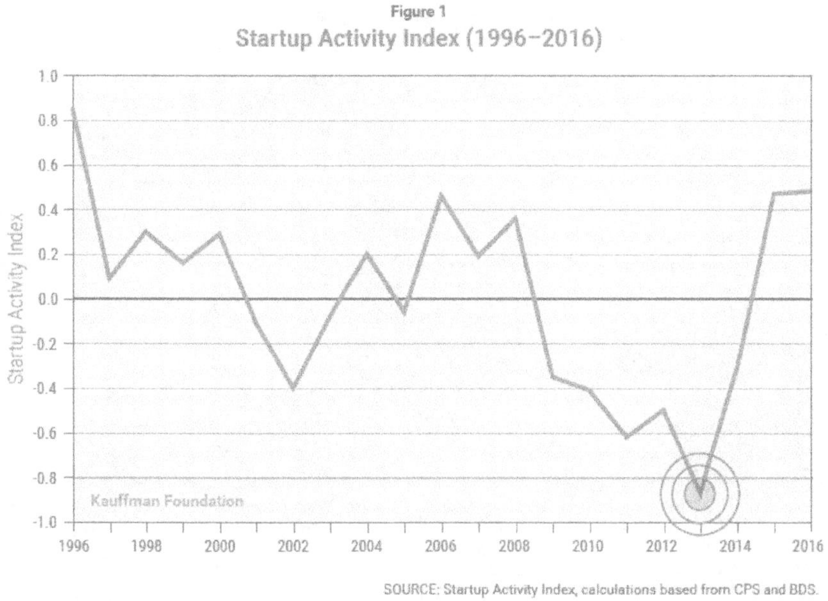

Figure 1
Startup Activity Index (1996–2016)

SOURCE: Startup Activity Index, calculations based from CPS and BDS.

As you would expect, after the economic crisis in 2008, there was a significant downturn in startup activity. Then in 2013, you'll notice a significant increase in startups again.

Second, I want to provide you an overview of the high-growth startup sectors. These are detailed on the next page. It's no surprise that software and IT services are in the top ten. However, outside of software, which is rated fifth, none of the other top ten are Business-to-Consumer (B2C) companies. Eight of the top ten are Business-to-Business (B2B) and one is Business-to-Government (B2G) service.

2016 Kauffman Index National Growth Entrepreneurship

Table C	Industries by Share of High-Growth Companies (2015)		
Rank	Industry	High-Growth Companies	Share (%)
1	IT Services	521	13.0%
2	Advertising & Marketing	397	9.9%
3	Business Products & Services	367	9.2%
4	Health	315	7.9%
5	Software	289	7.2%
6	Financial Services	195	4.9%
7	Construction	195	4.9%
8	Government Services	193	4.8%
9	Consumer Products & Services	188	4.7%
10	Human Resources	147	3.7%
11	Real Estate	134	3.3%
12	Retail	131	3.3%
13	Food & Beverage	123	3.1%
14	Logistics & Transportation	113	2.8%
15	Manufacturing	111	2.8%
16	Telecommunications	89	2.2%
17	Energy	88	2.2%
18	Security	71	1.8%
19	Engineering	63	1.6%
20	Education	58	1.4%
21	Insurance	55	1.4%
22	Travel & Hospitality	52	1.3%
23	Media	51	1.3%
24	Environmental Services	39	1.0%
25	Computer Hardware	23	0.6%

Source: Authors' calculations from Inc. 500|5000 data.

So, why do B2B firms dominate the top ten? B2B firms tend to generate revenue more rapidly than B2C firms. When B2B firms show growth and revenue, they can more easily attract investment. The B2B entrepreneurs have reduced the risk for investment in that particular startup. Secondly, B2B firms are typically launched by entrepreneurs with experience in that particular sector. Such experience often provides the entrepreneur with insights into problems that have been validated in that sector. The sector experience also provides the opportunity to build a personal network of people who can serve as fellow startup team members. Lastly, these entrepreneurs also have knowledge or even relationships with the prospective customers of their future startups. (See Step 6 - Law School for Your Startup.)

Interestingly, U.S. culture impacts those sectors which tend to be deemed more investable. For example, in the Midwest, where investors tend to be more risk averse than on the coasts, you will frequently see angel investors, startup accelerators and venture capital firms focus their investments more on B2B startups (which, as just mentioned, are inherently less risky than B2C startups). As you travel to the coasts (especially in San Francisco, New York and Boston), you find investors that are more risk tolerant. Therefore, these investors and startup accelerators are more willing to dedicate a larger portion of their investments in B2C firms. In Washington DC, as you can imagine, you find a greater commitment of investment capital directed to B2G startups, based on the experience and insights from those with government expertise.

Delusional Optimism ... it's a Beautiful Thing

I would be remiss to not discuss survival rates with you. It is very important to enter the world of startups with your eyes wide open. Startup survival rates are very low. Depending on the source, only 5-10 percent of startups are still in business after three years.

However, there is good news ...

"Hidden in much of the gloomy news about small business in recent years is an important positive statistic: business failure rates are in a long-term decline. The rate at which American employers go under has fallen by 30 percent since 1977."

Source: Scott Shane, Entrepreneur Magazine, January 2017

Nobel laureate in Economics and Professor from the University of Chicago at the Booth School of Business Daniel Kahneman shared during an interview with Inc's Eric Schurenberg:

"If you rationally weighed the odds of success, you'd never start a business. Thank goodness for irrationality. The good things in life, the major inventions, the major movements, came from people that, in a sense, didn't know the odds they were facing...One of the key traits of successful entrepreneurs is delusional optimism. Successful entrepreneurs have that optimism."

STEP
01

Assessing Your True Motivations

Step 1 – Assessing Your True Motivations

Brad Feld on what motivates entrepreneurs of thriving startups

It is appropriate to kick off the core content with insights from one of the most startup investors of all time, Brad Feld. Brad is one of the greatest minds in the field of entrepreneurship. If you are not familiar with him, he co-founded TechStars. TechStars has accepted over thousands of companies into its startup accelerator programs to date with an average acceptance rate of less than 1 percent per program. Collectively, these companies have raised over $3.3 billion USD and have a market cap of over $8.1 billion. (Source: TechStars, Wikipedia) Brad co-founded venture capital firm, Foundry Group, which has had five $225 million funds to date and one $500 million fund. He has written a series of books on entrepreneurship and venture capital. Brad regularly blogs on FeldThoughts.com.

I asked Brad to share his insights into the motivations of entrepreneurs who create thriving startups. This is the first of two areas we discussed.

"I learned a long time ago that there is a huge difference between the need for achievement (getting something done) and the need for independence (being your own boss). I first heard this from Ed Roberts at MIT in the early 1990s. My own experience is that entrepreneurs who have a need for achievement end up being much more successful in general than those who have a need for independence. These are not mutually independent things; you can have both, but one usually dominates."

Defining what Success Looks Like for You

Frankly, you wouldn't be reading this book if you simply wanted to finish your college degree and just get a regular job. You might have started your own business when you were in middle school, your parents might have their own successful company, you might like the idea of "wanting to be your own boss," "create your own future," or maybe you have a product or service idea that will help change people's lives.

So, you know why you are considering this journey, but what does success look like as your end goal for you personally? You need to define what success looks like to you—besides the money and everything you can purchase with it.

Now is a good time to write a minimum of three ways you will know you are personally being successful with your startup.

1)

2)

3)

Once you have identified what will make you personally feel successful as an entrepreneur, hang on to those. Come back to this list when times are tough, when you need to balance personal relationships, classes and your startup, when you have to fire a college friend from your startup, when customers don't pay you, when you discover your software developer won't meet a deadline for a customer when you run out of money.

WHEN YOU ASK YOURSELF, *IS THIS ALL REALLY WORTH IT?*

When Failure = Success

I continued my interview with Brad Feld and asked about how he sees successful entrepreneurs "recovering" and moving forward personally and professionally after a startup shuts down.

"A successful company is a compounded number of experiments, many of which fail. You have to learn from each of the failures. If you stand back and think of an entrepreneurial life, it usually consists of more than one company. Most entrepreneurs have both success and failure in their past, so this is often a helpful perspective in reframing the notion of failure."

I find it helpful when working with college-student entrepreneurs not only to talk about what success looks like, but also to envision where they have failed. We need to reframe what the traditional business world sees as failure and instead shift to an entrepreneurial mindset. By doing that, we can liberate ourselves from the inherent and logical fear of shutting down our startup. I have personally shut down two of my four startups, but I have learned from those experiences.

My first shut down where I had a significant equity stake cost me $55,000 in salary (I went six months without a paycheck) in addition to a $30,000 upfront investment. It cost my business partner $25,000 in deferred earnings and cost our investors hundreds of thousands of dollars.

Our investors, understandably, were not happy about losing their investment, but they ended up owning the software and IP (Intellectual Property)..

Incidentally, to this day, I still feel personal pain that they not only lost their investment, but did not get a spectacular return they deserved.

My business partner's $25k loss impacted his short-term finances. However, launching the startup caused him to reframe his future career choices. He discovered that he could not stomach the idea of going to work for a traditional organization again and instead, needed to launch another firm or be a partner in an existing firm (he chose the latter and is very satisfied with his choice).

I personally lost $85,000 in salary and upfront investment combined. However, I discovered a personal inner passion to always be engaged in some way, shape or form with a startup, and I knew my future startups needed to have purpose beyond financial achievement

Needless to say, it is difficult to foreshadow what you will learn from your startup journey, but if you can identify ways in which you can succeed, even if you shut down your startup, it will free you from some of the debilitating fears entrepreneurs face throughout their journeys.

Startup Insight: Don't let others project upon you what "success" looks like. Define your success. Even if you shut down your startup, you will learn things that other non-entrepreneurs will never learn.

Your Exit Options

You might be saying, "Wait a second Gee, you are supposed to be helping me launch my college startup, not shut it down." However, successful entrepreneurs that have identified all of their potential exit options *before launching their startups* in order to stay focused on long-term goals, reduce their own stress, reduce their family's stress, save time, and save money.

Here are some additional benefits to identifying your exit options before you begin:

1) Think about exit option decisions early.
2) Help make good hiring decisions.
3) Determine whether or not to take on investors and what type of investors you wish to select.
4) Define the maximum personal investment you and/or your family members are willing to make in your startup.
5) Set specific goals at which point you might sell your startup.
6) Decide the criteria that would make you shut down your startup.

There are essentially four ways that companies and owners exit:

1) **Merger or acquisition** – Mergers and acquisitions typically take place when it is more efficient and/or effective for another company to purchase your firm than it is for them to create their own products and services to compete with your firm. Selling the business is a common financial goal of those launching highly scalable startups while taking on investment capital. Whether you retain 100 percent ownership of your company or have investors, both situations desire returns on investment. Acquisition is the outcome that most angel investors and VCs seek in order to get a return on their investment.

2) **Initial Public Offering (IPO)** – IPOs used to be the ultimate goal of many startup founders. The odds of an IPO are extremely long; however, you or your investors might see it as a long-term, big payday. Many entrepreneurs have found that the glory of the IPO is overshadowed by

the scrutiny of thousands of individual investors. In general, these individual investors tend to focus on short-term objectives. This investor short-term focus makes it challenging for entrepreneurs to focus on requirements for long-term growth.

3) **Licensing** – You might find yourself in a situation where another company wants to license your intellectual property (IP) from you, but does not want your entire operation. For example, you might decide to shut down your company and move to a licensing model to provide ongoing personal revenue. Licensing provides the benefit of providing ongoing cash flow for you without the time commitment of managing day-to-day operations.

4) **Shut-down** – The day might come when you shut down your business with minimal or no financial benefit. Identifying now what events (e.g. specific maximum amount of capital invested, specific number of years, minimum amount of personal income from the business) will trigger you to close the business will help make that decision easier if the day comes. Those who tend to hang on too long, much like staying in a personal relationship that is doomed to fail, end up wasting time, wasting money and creating stress for the entrepreneur and their family.

Alright, now that we have a clear idea of all of our different exit options, let's get back to your startup idea.

STEP 02

Validating Your Startup Idea & Building Your Business Model

Step 2 – Validating Your Startup Idea & Building Your Business Model

Common truths about successful startup ideas

I hear new startup ideas every day from college students. Some are well-conceived, with a very creative new product or service with a significant market opportunity. They might even understand their market, have clearly identified a problem and have identified an idea that could fix that problem. Others might want to open a coffee shop, bar or restaurant without considering the hundreds of thousands of dollars needed before they even open for business, let alone the on-going costs of employees, rent, food, drinks and more. I frequently hear ideas about the latest social media app, without consideration that the average amount spent on marketing to gain initial traction, on average $5 million. I apologize if I have just crushed your startup idea but I might have saved you hundreds of thousands of dollars and years of your life. You still got your money's worth out of this book. ☺

I interviewed Chris Roche to discuss insights on the importance of conducting research before you launch your startup. Chris Roche is from Manchester, England. He came to the U.S. to play on the UW-Whitewater soccer team and complete his college degree. While at school, Chris launched Recruit Chute, an online platform that connects elite high school aged athletes with universities and colleges of their choice.

"The biggest thing that I see new entrepreneurs do wrong is that they build their product or service before finding out if there is any demand. You need to validate that people will actually purchase your product before you spend any money. I wish we had just created screenshots or basic landing pages before developing our initial software application. Our RecruitChute user growth has really accelerated since we A/B tested different designs selected the most widely adopted version. THEN we moved into developing our full commercial level platform."

Sometimes ideas are a solution in search of a problem.

Entrepreneurs in search of a problem, aka using a "build it and they will come" strategy, are typically a recipe for an epic startup train wreck.

Here are some of the common truths I have found to be true about successful startup ideas (notice we talk about startup *ideas*, because if the startup does not have users, it is still just an idea):

When diving into unfamiliar waters have a buddy – Diving into a market in which you have no experience puts you at an immediate disadvantage. You are competing in a market with refined businesses models, large networks of connected people and organizations, barriers to entry which might be obvious and others that aren't, and legal ramifications with which you are not familiar. However, many students don't have that expertise, that is ok there are ways to overcome that lack of expertise.

There are some ways to overcome the lack of familiarity with a market:

- Locate other founding team members or advisors that do have the experience.
- Conduct a significant amount of research about that market.

I am not saying there isn't room for market disruptors, with little experience in the market they are entering There are those who have successfully upended markets with which they had little familiarity such as: Richard Branson with almost all of his Virgin brands, Elon Musk with Tesla, and Herb Kelleher with Southwest Airlines. However, these visionaries were wise enough to find the best people in the applicable sectors to help them disrupt markets.

Is there a true "pain point" you are addressing? Sure, many products and services exist that can increase convenience and make life more enjoyable. But in general, those ideas that address true pain points will be most rapidly adopted (purchased by your customers).

People and businesses are willing to spend more money on products and services that provide benefits including, but not limited to:

- Saving time
- Saving money
- Increasing productivity
- Increasing profit
- Increasing safety

Many products we purchase and use every day are simply conveniences. For example, I enjoy using my Google Home speaker every day as well as my iPhone. But the amount of work and money that Google and Apple had to devote toward building brand awareness, communicating that "convenience" and providing the sales channels to distribute it are significant. Typically, this is money that the average college student startup does not have.

Startup Insight: If your product or service can address a pain point and you can clearly articulate how you can address that pain point, you will speed up your market adoption and increase the likelihood of your success.

The Competition

If you want to immediately lose credibility with prospective customers, team members, your entrepreneurship professors, prospective investors, future employees, other entrepreneurs and industry experts, tell them "I don't have any competition." You will get eye rolling, head shaking and sometimes people just burying their forehead in the palms of their hands.

All products and services face some kind of competition. When college-student entrepreneurs ask me the question, "How do I know if I have any competition?" I recommend they go to this little-known website: Google.com to begin. This is in addition to the resources most likely available at your college like: Lexis Nexus, Statista, Alexa, Info USA and Dun and Bradstreet. The insights from these secondary research sources can save you a significant amount of time, money and aggravation. Take the time to use them.

Analyzing the Competition

Two helpful tools when analyzing your competitive environment are a SWOT analysis and Porter's Five Forces Model.

SWOT – SWOT is an acronym for Strengths, Weaknesses, Opportunities and Threats. A SWOT analysis can help you analyze your startup idea relative to both macro and micro environmental factors. Macro environmental factors include: political factors, demographic social factors, competitive factors, legal factors and natural factors (as in our world). Micro environmental factors include: customers, employees, distribution channels and suppliers, competitors, investors, media and the general public.

When creating your SWOT, consider the following:

Startup Idea Strengths: What strengths will your startup idea have relative to other competitors? Focus on sustainable competitive advantages, not just an advantage you have the day of launch. Avoid falling into the classic trap of saying, "we are cheaper." Being lower priced is easy when you are a small organization with no overhead, but as your costs increase, your margins will decrease and you will lose your "competitive strength."

Startup Idea Weaknesses: Identify weaknesses in your business model that will be difficult to overcome, at least initially. Avoid the trap here of saying, "we have none." Take the time to identify weaknesses. Once the weaknesses are identified, you can try to minimize those weaknesses as you roll out and scale your business.

Startup Idea Opportunities: What opportunities exist in the market that are based on problems you plan to solve or other unmet needs? Ideally, these are opportunities that the incumbent players (your future competitors) have not yet identified and ideally would not have the capability to meet. The opportunity drives your value proposition. Think about long-term as well as short-term opportunities. Perhaps look for changes in laws that could assist you, growth of new sectors in the economy, competitors that might go out of business, etc.

Startup Idea Threats: What threats will you face in the short and long term that could significantly diminish your capacity to grow or put you out of business? The threats could come from competitors, access to capital, changes in the economy, environmental factors, not being able to find cost-effective talent, a limited number of suppliers, technology changes, etc.

Create your SWOT here:

Strengths	Weaknesses
Opportunities	Threats

Porter's Five Forces Model

Porter's Five Forces Model was developed by Michael Porter from Harvard. This model helps us define the sources of competition at a more micro environmental level. The focus is on five forces that determine the competitive intensity and, therefore, the attractiveness (or lack of it) of an industry in terms of its profitability.

To use Porter's Five Forces model, you need to work through these questions for each area:

1. Threat of New Entry?
2. Buyer Power?
3. Threat of Substitution?
4. Supplier Power?
5. Competitive Rivalry?

Threat of New Entry

If a new business can easily be started up in your sector without substantial investment, then this is a threat.

- What's the threat of new businesses starting in this sector?
- How easy is it to start up in this business?
- What are the rules and regulations?
- What finances would be needed to begin a startup?
- Are there barriers to entry which give you greater power?

Buyer Power

Where there are fewer buyers, they often control the market. Questions here include:

- How powerful are the buyers?
- How many are there?
- Can the buyers get costs down?
- Do they have the power to dictate terms?

Threat of Substitution

If there are available alternatives, then the threat of substitution increases.

- How easy is it to find an alternative to this product or service?
- Can it be outsourced? Automated?

Supplier Power

In markets where few suppliers exist, the suppliers retain the power.

- How many suppliers are in the market?
- Are there a few who control prices?
- Are there many suppliers, so prices are lower?
- Do your suppliers hold the power?
- How easy is it to switch? What's the cost?

Competitive Rivalry

Markets where there are few competitors are attractive, but can be short-lived. In highly competitive markets with many companies chasing the same work, it reduces your power in the market.

- What's the level of competition in this sector?
- What's the competitor situation? Are there many competitors causing all of you to be in a commodity situation, or are there just a few?

Source: Michael E. Porter, Porter's Five Forces, Harvard Business Review

Why are YOU the person who should address the pain point?

You might have determined there is a pain point in your market, and may have even discovered that your solution addresses the problem. But, you also need to think about why *you* are the person to address the issue.

Hopefully, you can answer "yes" to a minimum of three of the following:

1. Do you have a unique product or service that is very difficult to copy?
2. Do you, your team members or advisors have special insights?
3. Can you get to market more quickly than others?
4. Have you demonstrated your ability to engage these customers before?
5. Could you build a team of experts that would be difficult to replicate?
6. Do you have the risk tolerance necessary to succeed?

Angel investor Ross Leinweber and I had an interesting discussion where he shared his thoughts about risk tolerance, relative to cultural dispositions.

"Risk tolerance is a multi-factor concept, however, subtle ideas of how a population was brought to an area, what their natural cultural tendencies exhibit, have profound long-term effects on risk taking in general on the direct population and their descendants. Examples include the gold rush in California, or immigrants using a raft to cross the Mediterranean Sea. These are both great anecdotes to say these people wanted a better life … willing to literally risk their lives for it, so the idea of a failing business is no big deal for someone that has experienced that. These are extreme examples, but they showcase the phenomena.

However, if a first-time founder launches later on in life, they have more capital of their own to invest and easier access to outside capital. These people also have a much higher opportunity cost (the loss of their previous salary). In addition to financial risk, some consider in advance the reputational risk—especially if this is their first startup. They get concerned about how they will be perceived by their peers, future employers, etc. I think one of the reasons there are so many startups in California is cultural. The first people who arrived in California risked everything in pursuit of finding gold, and you see that tolerance of risk playing out. This same behavior and risk tolerance are evident in immigrants, who launch companies at a much higher rate than current citizens. If they were willing to risk everything and move to create a better life, then starting a new business has a relatively small element of risk.

Lastly, I have found that risk taking can be learned. Even if you are not generally risk tolerant, if you are surrounded by people taking risks, that tolerance for risk rubs off. It can become a learned behavior."

Market Discovery – Go Get the Truth

Until you have users (consuming the product or service but not paying for it) and ideally customers (usually users of the product or service who are paying for it) gaining benefit from your product or service, you still have a "startup idea."

Startup ideas are very personal, especially if you have spent a great deal of time generating the idea and are contemplating dedicating a career to the startup idea. Entrepreneurs get less defensive over time as they launch subsequent startups. You may try to avoid people that might give you news you don't want to hear, but that aversion can also doom your startup idea. You need to go out and seek the truth.

One of my favorite movies of all time is, *A Few Good Men*. The film is a military drama with a final intense courtroom scene between Tom Cruise and Jack Nicholson. During the final courtroom scene, where Jack Nicholson is getting grilled on the stand by Tom Cruise, he yells from the top of his lungs…

"You can't handle the truth."

You too need to "find the truth" about whether you have a viable startup idea. So, get out of your dorm room or apartment, and, to go and talk to people that might buy your product or service if it was available to them. It might seem scary at first but you will eventually find out that this is actually quite fun…if you take it as an opportunity to learn, to meet new people and perhaps even to find future customers. Avoid getting defensive, although this can be difficult, because at some point our startups become very personal.

Criticisms of our startup ideas can be construed as criticisms of us but you need to relentlessly move forward, learning and refining your startup idea as you.

You will eventually master the skill of going out and conducting market discovery. You will find that many people like to talk with budding entrepreneurs ... sometimes because they are jealous that you had the guts to make the jump into the world of entrepreneurship and they didn't. Good for you!

Asking your friends and family members if they like your idea and how much they would pay for the idea is **not** a sound marketing research strategy. In fact, it is probably a recipe for disaster. Friends and family, in general, are an easy source for feedback, but they are not a representative sample of prospective customers. Quite frankly, they are going to tell you whatever you want to hear, or if they don't want you to take the risk, they will be too cynical.

You need to spend a significant amount of time talking to a random sample of real prospective customers with whom you have no relationship in order to get the cold hard truth about your idea. Talk with people you don't know. Talk with potential buyers living throughout the country or the world.

I spoke with Troy Vosseller, one of the founders of gener8tor. gener8tor is a nationally ranked startup accelerator. Troy provided critical insights about sharing your startup idea.

"One of the traps I see first-time entrepreneurs fall into with great frequency is being afraid to talk about their idea. There are over 7 billion people currently in the world. You are naïve to think that you are the only one who has ever had this idea. The best way to find out if there is a market for your idea is to talk openly and honestly to get the feedback and resources you need to successfully execute your idea.

When first-time entrepreneurs develop their first startup idea, they frequently become paranoid about others "stealing" their ideas. Sure, you can ask people to sign an NDA (nondisclosure agreement) as a layer of protection. Be prepared that some of the most insightful people you will talk with along your entrepreneurial journey will not be willing to sign NDAs. Startup mentors, angel investors, accelerator managers and others hear so many ideas that they are not going to expose themselves to liability in the event they hear a similar idea in the future, if that person has a better execution plan.

Startup Insight: Share your idea with as many prospective paying customers as you can to refine your startup and let go of the paranoia of someone "stealing your idea." Startup success is not driven by the idea itself, but by the execution of the idea.

Market Discovery Questions

Next, we need to create the questions for our market discovery. A helpful tool when creating these questions is using a Solution Map. As you can see below, we are focused on the area between the customer's current situation and the ideal situation. We are trying to solve the pain point with our solution (startup idea).

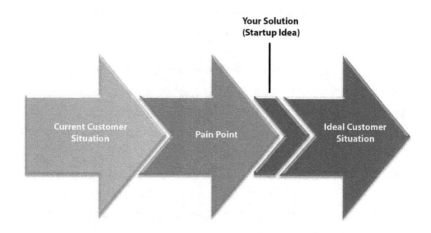

Initial Hypotheses

When we begin with our startup idea, we have many hypotheses (theories about our startup idea). However, we can't presume that our hypotheses are reality. We need to spend the time to invalidate/validate these hypotheses or risk wasting an incredible amount of time and money.

Let's say we had a startup idea for an electricity saving service connected to a mobile application. Here are some of our possible hypotheses:

1. Consumers feel they spend too much on electricity.
2. Consumers do not have an easy way to monitor their own electricity consumption.
3. Consumers would like a mobile app where they can monitor their electricity consumption in real time.

4. Consumers would be willing to pay $4.99 for the app download and $2.99/month.
5. We should launch the app first in the App Store.
6. Consumers would primarily like to learn about us through their electric company.
7. The electric company would like to promote our mobile app to help reduce customer calls when customer bills arrive.
8. The electric company will want to "white label" our mobile app.
9. Our cost to develop our mobile app will be under $25k.
10. Our cost to develop the hardware to integrate with home thermostats will be under $50k.
11. Our installation will be provided by certified electricians throughout the U.S.
12. Our first beta markets should be New York and Boston.
13. We will be able to patent our technology.
14. Our first-year operating budget will be under $150,000.

Discovery Questions

Before we jump into specific market discovery questions to test our hypotheses, let's review the two forms of questions and the benefits of using each question.

Open-ended questions – Open-ended questions are questions used to elicit an open, free response. Open-ended questions yield a great deal of information. We want to focus our discovery interviews on open-ended questions, especially at the beginning of the discovery interview. Not only does starting with the discovery meeting help us get a big picture of their current situation at the beginning, it also helps get the prospective customer to open up to us.

Open-ended questions begin with words such as:

- What
- Why
- Will
- How
- Where
- Describe
- Tell

Closed-ended questions – Closed-ended questions are questions used to refine understanding of the situation. Closed-ended questions typically yield brief answers such as a yes or no, or other specific responses. These questions should be answered later in the discovery interview.

Closed-ended questions begin with words such as:

- Do
- Can
- Where
- Does
- Did
- Could
- Should
- Is
- Are
- Have

Market discovery interviews are a blend of both open-ended and closed-ended questions. A helpful process to use when conducting discovery research is a method called the **funnel approach**. The concept behind the funnel approach is that you get the most comprehensive information when you ask a combination of open- and closed-ended questions, in that order. Quick pointer here: This is also the best method to use when finding out customers' needs when you are ready to begin selling your product or service.

FUNNEL APPROACH

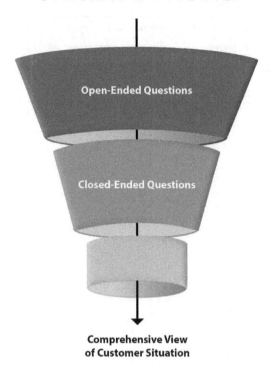

Open-Ended Questions

Closed-Ended Questions

**Comprehensive View
of Customer Situation**

Spending time conducting initial discovery research through electronic surveys is a bad idea. You need to capture a wide variety of information from these people. Utilizing these surveys means you are essentially using closed-ended questions, which prevent you from gathering the range of information you need. Closed-ended questions often tend to be leading questions.

If you cannot meet with potential customers face-to-face, you might try via webinar or video chat. This gives you an opportunity to read body language and provides other benefits, such as gaining insights from the customer's environment too. If you have the money, use a professional service like WebEx. Some universities will have a service such as WebEx that they will let students use for free. If you are on a strict budget, use Skype or Google Hangouts. Keep in mind, if you have prospective customers who are going to be spending a great deal of money with you (e.g. a B2B client), spend the money for the professional webinar service. Making a great first impression with these people is critical.

Startup Insight: Don't just ask leading questions when conducting discovery. Ask the questions that will validate or invalidate your hypotheses by using open- and closed-ended questions. These are the questions that will help increase the likelihood of you launching a successful startup.

Resist the temptation of sharing your solution (startup idea) in the discovery interview until you are comfortable that you have a comprehensive view of the customer's current situation. If you share it too early you will simply bias people's answers and make false assumptions that could be fatal to your startup.

Here are some examples of the most critical customer situational questions you need to ask:

Customer Situational Questions

1. Describe your current situation relative to _____.
2. What is currently working well for you?
3. What challenges or problems are you facing?
4. What solutions are you using to solve those problems?
5. Where did you find out about those solutions?
6. How well are those solutions working for you?
7. Are you aware of any other solutions?
8. Why have you not looked at other solutions?
9. How much do you pay for the current solution?
10. How do you feel about the amount you are paying?
11. What would the ideal solution look like to you?
12. Would you be willing to consider a new solution?
13. Where would you most likely learn about the new solution?
14. What would convince you that the new solution would fix the problem?

Write down a few customer situational questions for your startup idea here:

1.

2.

3.

4.

5.

6.

7.

8.

9.

10.

Solution-Specific Questions

Once you have completed your customer situational-specific questions, you can present your solution, followed by asking solution-specific questions. Avoid pitching them on why they should select your solution. This is very difficult to do, given that you might already have an emotional connection to your startup idea. Here are sample questions you could ask:

1. What do you think of _____ (your solution)?
2. What do you specifically like about the solution?
3. What do you dislike about the solution?
4. What would you change about the solution?
5. Where would you most likely learn about this solution?
6. What specific sources would you trust to validate that this solution would work?
7. Would you purchase this solution?
8. Where would you want to purchase this solution?
9. How frequently would you purchase this solution?
10. How much would you pay for the solution?
11. Would you be willing to pre-pay for the solution?
12. What payment terms (e.g. net 30) would you be willing to accept?
13. Would you expect any specific warranties or guarantees? If yes, tell me about what those warranties or guarantees would look like.
14. Would you like to participate in our beta (if at this point you think you could generate substantial information from this prospective customer)?

Write down some of your solution-specific questions:

1.

2.

3.

4.

5.

6.

7.

8.

9.

10.

How many discovery questions should you ask?

I frequently get asked this question from college students, "Gee, how many people should I talk to in order to know if people want my product?" I will give you my academic answer first. "You should use a representative sample size of your population of customers." If you haven't taken a statistics class, a representative sample size is the number of people, organizations, etc. that you need to talk to in order to draw a reliable conclusion. You can use tools such as sample size calculators to determine a representative sample size."

Most college-student entrepreneurs don't have the time nor money to execute on a number that large. A rule of thumb that my fellow startup accelerator friends and I tend to live by is to talk with a random sample of a minimum of one hundred prospective customers. There are obvious exceptions. For example, if you are selling into a B2B market and the market size is relatively small, this might not be possible. What we find is that most new entrepreneurs will not talk to one hundred prospective customers. Then we think, "If they are not willing to talk to one hundred prospective customers how on earth will they launch and grow a successful startup?"

Once we determine how many prospective customers have been surveyed, we launch into seven key questions.

Teaser alert: It is no coincidence that these questions are the foundation of most startup pitch decks, which we will discuss later.

Questions that you can expect from those who might be mentoring you or investing in your startup.

1. Tell me about the market.
2. Tell me about the problem.
3. Tell me about your solution.
4. Tell me about your competition.
5. Tell me why you are better.
6. Tell me where you are in the startup cycle.
7. Tell me about your next steps.

It's Okay to Take It Out Back

Conducting this research through asking discovery questions will help you refine your startup idea. Frankly, it might make you reconsider even proceeding with your idea. Killing an idea, or "taking it out back" (Old Yeller movie reference here — watch the movie if you haven't seen it. Spoiler alert it has a very sad ending) as I refer to the process, is a much better decision than dedicating years of your life and countless amounts of money to an idea that is destined for failure. Frankly, it is the humane thing to do.

So, yes, it's okay if "take it out back." You will naturally feel deflated; it can become very personal. However, entrepreneurs don't develop one idea or one startup and then stop. Usually, ideas will start emanating from their creative minds shortly after they decide not to pursue a startup idea. I personally have had over 100 ideas. I simply put them in the Notes app of my iPhone and come back to them if I think it has a true market opportunity. Then I go out and talk to prospective customers to see if there is indeed a pain point, how they are solving the problem and what they think of my solution.

First-time entrepreneurs might only have one idea, but over time you will generate many others. Some will be derived from your first startup idea. As time passes, entrepreneurs tend to become impervious to their startup shutting down; they simply move on to their next startup idea.

Startup Insight: Entrepreneurs don't usually give up after one startup idea that does not come to fruition. They dust themselves off, get back on their horse and continue to ride.

Determining your Market Size

Once you have gotten to the point where you are comfortable your solution (startup idea) addresses a real pain point, we need to determine the market size.

Simply said, is the market big enough to justify the money and time invested?

Before we move on, it is important to understand some more terminology to help identify our market opportunity.

Total Addressable Market (TAM) – Total number of customers in a particular market.

Serviceable Addressable Market (SAM) – Segment of the TAM that is targeted by your products/services.

Serviceable Obtainable Market (SOM) – Portion of the SAM that you can realistically capture.

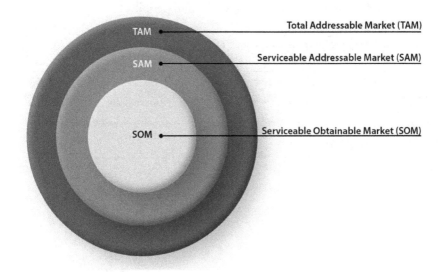

For the sake of illustration, I am going to create a fictional startup idea. This startup idea will be used to demonstrate analyzing the TAM, SAM and SOM.

We will also use this same example for the upcoming chapters on developing your brand and marketing.

Startup Idea: Let's say you have a startup idea which is comprised of software to coordinate in-home care for seniors. You might scope out the market in the following manner:

1. **The Total Addressable Market (TAM)** – There are currently 8,350,100 people in the U.S. who receive support from the five main long-term care services; home health agencies (4,742,500), nursing homes (1,383,700), hospices (1,244,500), residential care communities (713,300) and adult day care service centers (273,200).

2. **The Serviceable Addressable Market (SAM)** – Our software is targeted at those providing home health care. Therefore, our SAM is 4,742,500 people.

3. **Serviceable Obtainable Market (SOM)** – Perhaps we estimate that we can capture 1 percent of the market in the first three years. Therefore, the SOM would be 47,425 (1% x 4,742,500) people.

Data Source: Family Caregiver Alliance, Feb 2015

Startup Insight: You need to be very careful estimating the Serviceable Obtainable Market. The SOM can be used to show you have a grasp on market size, but it is important to be very conservative when estimating this number, especially if you decide to meet with prospective investors or pitch accelerators.

Developing a Solid Business Model

Idella Yamben is the Business Development Consultant for UW-Extension's Center for Technology Commercialization (CTC). She combines research and scientific acumen with her years of assisting high-tech entrepreneurs in HR and technology commercialization goals. She is also a member of an angel investment fund called The Frontier Fund, Idella champions Lean Startup principles as a tool to invite entrepreneurs of all types to participate in this exciting ecosystem.

Idella shared with me her insights on shifting from a "build it and they will come mentality" to focusing on a specific problem and translating that into a viable business model.

"I find that quite often an entrepreneur begins with the focus on the product. They might have a patent or may have received regulatory approval; they might even have solved a problem, but they haven't built a business model. They assume these steps lead directly to a paying customer, and are shocked when it does not. They have technical expertise, and believe the business part will just happen if they execute. You can imagine it is shocking for them to go from being an expert in their specific area of knowledge, to being humbled by how little they know when it comes to creating a viable business.

The Canvas tools, such as the Business Model Canvas – Canvanizer.com tool, create some order in all the chaos and unknown. The Business Model Canvas outlines nine critical elements giving the entrepreneur a logical discovery roadmap toward a viable business model. You first discover and validate significant problems for customers, and then you can validate the unique value your business offers. With the Canvas tools and use of Lean Startup methodology, there is a bit of a process to follow, making entrepreneurship more accessible and less mysterious."

Business models describe the methods that a business uses to create and deliver value to its customers. Taking the time to develop your initial business model can be critical to the life of your startup. Your business will evolve over time and as you "pivot" (change elements within your business model).

Traditional business model elements include:

- Value proposition
- Customer segments
- Revenue models
- Marketing and sales
- Business partner relationships
- Cost structure

In an effort to make the development of a business model more comprehensive, Alexander Osterwalder developed a graphical tool that helps entrepreneurs considerably. This tool is called the Business Model Canvas (BMC), which Idella previously referenced. This tool is not only well-respected at institutions including Stanford, MIT and University of Chicago, but is almost universally embraced by angel investors, startup accelerators and, most importantly, successful entrepreneurs. I require that my student entrepreneurs use this to develop an initial foundation for their business. It is a very helpful tool to help them guide their discovery.

You can watch a video demonstrating how the Business Model Canvas works by visiting this website: http://bit.ly/2i4bWDs

The Business Model Canvas includes nine key elements you need to define and refine as you move through the discovery process.

1. Value propositions
2. Customer segments
3. Customer relationships
4. Distribution channels
5. Key resources
6. Key activities
7. Key partners
8. Cost structure
9. Revenue streams

The Business Model Canvas

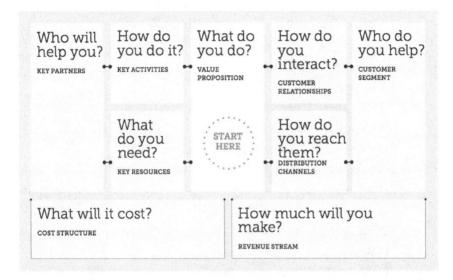

Source: Osterwalder A, Pigneur Y, Business Model Generation, 2010

You can see an example of a Business Model Canvas by going to startupguides.io and clicking on "Resources."

When developing your Business Model Canvas, the questions that need to be answered for each of the nine elements include (but are not limited to):

1. Customer Segments
   a. List all of your various customer segments (initial customer types and future types).
   b. I recommend including users in here as well—those who use your product but do not pay you.
2. Customer Relationships
   a. How are you going to interact with your customers?
   b. Where are some of your initial sources of prospects?
   c. How will you make the initial sale?
   d. What methods will you use to provide customer support?
3. Value Proposition

    a.   What value does your business provide the customer?

    b.   What is the customer problem you are solving?

    c.   Is there a sustainable competitive advantage?

    d.   How are you delivering the service?

4. Distribution (Sales) Channels

    a.   What sales channels will you use?

    b.   Which sales channels should you use first?

    c.   Which sales channels are the most effective?

    d.   Which sales channels are the most efficient?

5. Revenue Streams

    a.   How much are customers willing to pay you (based on your discovery)?

    b.   What methods do they want to use to pay you?

    c.   How frequently do they want to pay you?

    d.   Describe all of the potential revenue streams (note: only having one revenue stream is a recipe for disaster – think of multiple options).

6. Key Activities

    a.   Do you need to secure a patent?

    b.   Should you hire a software engineer as an independent contractor?

    c.   Do you need warehouse space?

    d.   When should you rent an office space?

7. Key Resources

    a.   What are the critical elements to your startup's success?

    b.   How many people do you need on your core development team?

    c.   Should you use direct or indirect sales channels?

    d.   How many delivery trucks do you need?

8. Key Partners

    a.   What is your priority market? Example: West Coast, Midwest and East Coast distributors.

    b.   Who should you select for your law firm?

    c.   Who should you select for your software development firm?

9. Cost Structure

    a.   What is your target cost of goods sold?

    b.   What is your cost of customer acquisition?

    c.   What will be your initial capital costs?

Business Model Canvas Tools

There are free web-based tools that I use with college-student entrepreneurs that you can use to create a Business Model Canvas for your startup idea.

Here are two of the FREE web-based tools I recommend entrepreneurs use:

1. Canvanizer - canvanizer.com

2. Strategyzer - strategyzer.com

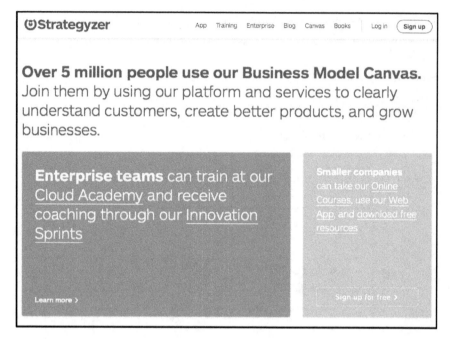

I spoke with Heidi Neck, Professor of Entrepreneurship at Babson College. Babson has been ranked the No. 1 undergraduate entrepreneurship program 18 times by U.S. News and World Report. I respect Heidi so much that I use her textbook in one of my classes. She referenced an element of her book regarding value propositions and the importance of them to entrepreneurs.

"I think it is easy for entrepreneurs to simply write down some features and functionality without considering the benefits provided to the customer. We should really reframe value proposition and instead use the term, customer value proposition. In my textbook, *Entrepreneurship Mindset and Practice*, we use the term customer value proposition because it reminds entrepreneurs that the focus should be on the customer first, and then on how that value yields a profit for the company."

Source: Entrepreneurship Mindset and Practice, Neck, Neck, Murray, 2017

STEP

03

Balancing Classes, Relationships and Your Startup

Step 3 – Balancing Classes, Relationships and Your Startup

How to Balance Classes, Relationships and Your Startup

I cringe when I hear college students who are contemplating launching a new business say that one of their motivations is to have free time to do what they want. If you talk with entrepreneurs who have launched and grown their businesses to the heights of success, you will not hear many tales of increased balance in their lives, at least during the early stages of their companies. Launching a successful startup takes a significant amount of time, energy, focus and commitment.

Balancing your classes, relationships, jobs, and your startup is no easy task. Whether you are an undergraduate student or graduate student, have a job or not, have a girlfriend or boyfriend, and even regardless of your major, launching a startup should be done with great care.

Let's explore strategies that have worked for student entrepreneurs.

I interviewed Jake Smith, a former student of mine who thrives on being on the cutting edge of new technologies and startups. Jake was a co-founder and former CEO of RankR Esports and is now an Operations Platform Administrator at Bird (the electric scooter company). Jake shared his insights about how he cleverly managed his startup and his classes, studied abroad, raised $400k in startup funding, and eventually landed a job with the fastest growing startup of all time.

"I personally always viewed balancing school and my startup pretty one-sided – focus on the startup. I also wanted to leverage all the knowledge I could from school, too. I was going into my senior year at UW-Whitewater when I came up with the idea for RankR Esports, an Esports virtual hub, so I knew I just had to get through my classes and still launch the startup.

I had to figure out how to combine my startup and school early on, so the first semester of my senior year, I moved to Korea to study Esports. After returning, I had a lot of lessons to learn in order to be both a student and a CEO/Founder.

While I focused on my startup, there was still a lot of work I had to do for my classes. While the last semester may "feel like a victory lap," especially when your startup already has funding, you still have to get it done. At the beginning of that last semester I had a lot of sleepless nights because I didn't have strong enough time-management skills. I learned really quickly how important those skills were and now I use them every day. The ability to prioritize based on both urgency and required time is invaluable, especially when you are in a high-growth situation. I was one of the first 20 employees at Bird and have since moved to managing a lot of our global platforms. The skills I learned during my startup are a large part of my career and need to be constantly honed if you want to have a real impact on the success of a fast growth company, whether it is your firm, another startup, or an early stage company."

Now, it's time to discuss the inevitable question of prioritization - of classes, jobs, relationships, and more. (we will discuss the ultimate decision of startup vs. college in Step 12).

When you arrived as a freshman in college, inevitably, you were excited but also might have faced a time of chaos and some fear of the unknown.

Some of your questions might have included:

- Will I get along with my roommate?
- How difficult will my classes be?
- Will I like my classes?
- What will my eventual major be?
- How will I pay for college?
- How will I balance sports with my classes?
- Should I join a fraternity or sorority?

- How involved should I get with college organizations?
- Will I find a boyfriend of girlfriend?
- When will I graduate?

The list goes on and on. Eventually, the fears you started with fade and your path becomes clearer. We see most college students launching startups in their junior or senior years, but I have worked with freshmen and sophomores who have launched highly successful startups, too.

Priorities shift and change throughout life, not just during college. You will find that there is a constant battle between personal relationships, your career, finances, enjoying hobbies and other activities. Believe it or not, when you are at college, these choices tend to be a little easier - more black and white.

So, ask yourself the following questions before you launch your startup:

- What are my *real* priorities?
- How will I use my time to drive those priorities?
- Will I have to let something go to achieve my goals?

Every semester, students who are conducting discovery on their startup idea, launching their startup, or growing a startup, come into my office with a similar concern. The conversation usually goes something like this:

Me: "So, how are things going?"

Student Entrepreneur: "Ok." [Said unconvincingly.]

Me: "Why don't you grab the door. [Door closes.] Now, how are things *really* going?"

Student Entrepreneur: "My startup is going fine but I just bombed my (fill in class name here) exam."

Me: "What happened?"

Student Entrepreneur: "I am spending all my time working on my startup. I am not paying attention in class. I sit in the back of the classroom on my laptop working on my startup."

Me: "How much time are you putting into your startup per week?"

Student Entrepreneur: "I don't know, 30 or 40 hours."

Me: "How much time are you studying?"

Student Entrepreneur: "Probably 10." [This is usually an exaggeration.]

Me: "So, what will happen if you continue down this path?"

Student Entrepreneur: "I will probably flunk out."

Me: "Alright, so what if that happens?"

Student Entrepreneur: "My parents will kill me. They will be so disappointed."

Me: "Anything else?"

The conversation then leads various directions depending on how far the student is along in school, their major, their GPA, motivations for going to college, the success of their startup, etc. Then we continue with the best path, which can also go in many different directions. We will explore these directions and options in Step 12: Should I stay or should I go.

You will notice I did not tell them what to do. I simply used the Socratic method to helping them through their dilemma. If you haven't taken a psychology class, the Socratic method is named for the early Greek philosopher/teacher Socrates. The Socratic method of teaching is one in which the instructor poses thoughtful questions to help students learn. Interestingly, this is the same approach used in behavioral therapy, the premise being that people commit themselves to resolving problems in life when they identify the problems themselves and also develop their own solutions. There will not be a quiz on this later.

Alright, let's get back to your priorities. Ultimately, determining YOUR priorities is a decision YOU will need to make. No one can make them for you, not your parents, not your professors, not your boyfriend or girlfriend, not your friends, not your student org peers. If you want to be truly satisfied in the long run, you need to identify your own priorities.

I have created a model to help you determine your priorities. I call this model the 5S model. Use "Specific Situation" to include other priorities in your world, such as a job you have during school.

5S Model Exercise

Rank each of these facets of your life from 1 to 5 (1=Most Important and 5=Least Important).

Be honest with yourself. Do not answer based on outside pressures, but what you truly feel are your priorities.

_____ Social relationships

_____ School

_____ Startup

_____ Salary (current income)

_____ Specific situation (provide details) _____

Take Action

Dedicate your time to #1 and #2. Realize that #3 will need to take a back seat and that #4 or #5 might need to go. This could be a brutal realization. Unfortunately, sometimes that might be a personal relationship. I have seen personal relationships and even marriages end because of the demands of the startup life.

It is critical to have candid, heart-to-heart conversations with the people you care about so that they're aware that you are going to be committing a great deal of time to your startup and it will indeed mean less time with them. If they know this when you begin your startup life, it can lead to a great deal less resentment and increase the probability that you will be able to maintain that relationship and still launch your startup.

It probably goes without saying, but these priorities can shift over time. Whenever you feel stressed about your time and shifting priorities, come back to the list and re-rank your priorities. It will help provide you focus.

On the topic of relationships, it is important to consider who you are spending your time with during college. These people can have a significant impact on your life and your startup.

I interviewed Henry Schwartz, one of the founders and CEO of Mobcraft Beer. Henry founded Mobcraft when he determined that anyone, regardless of age, could buy **ingredients** for beer. So, Henry started brewing beer and having friends over for a "small sampling." Then his friends starting adding crazy ingredients like jalapenos and chocolate. Eventually, Henry and his co-founders built a website where people could submit recipes for beer, then push out requests through social media accounts for their friends to "vote" on their recipe. Mobcraft experienced tremendous growth, to the point where Henry eventually was a contestant on ABC's *Shark Tank*. He now has his own brewery which sells their crowd-sourced beers to retailers, and he continues his creative website business.

Henry developed a strategy that I see most creative college-student entrepreneurs now employing. In fact, I allow student entrepreneurs to use this strategy in my entrepreneurship classes.

Here are Henry's thoughts…

"Rather than see classes at college as an obstacle to building a successful startup, I saw them as complementary. I actually used the needs of my startup to fulfill the requirements of classes. In one of my Spanish classes, I took the copy from an advertising campaign and translated it into Spanish as a project. Mobcraft needed a logo and designs for beer labels. I talked to my graphic design professor about having our logo designed and beer labels designed as a project for graphic design students. He loved the idea. We explained the requirements to students and then selected the best designs. Two of those students actually still work for us at Mobcraft.

In my entrepreneurship courses I would ask the professors if I could use my startup as the basis for my class project work. They were more than happy to oblige. They wanted to see me immediately apply the knowledge from their classes and I would give updates on Mobcraft in class. So, students got to learn from a living, breathing startup."

College-student entrepreneurs frequently find that the people they spent their time with *prior* to having their startup and the people they spend time with *afterwards* are a completely different group of people. This does not happen by accident. As your startup moves forward, you will become selective of the people with whom you spend time. And, frequently, it will be people who can relate to your startup life and help move your startup forward.

I next interviewed Brandon Fong. Of all the students I've worked with, I have never met anyone that developed such a mastery of time management and networking while in college as perfectly as Brandon did. While at UW-Whitewater, Brandon launched his first startup company, published a book, studied abroad twice, and graduated with a double major in entrepreneurship and marketing. Brandon shared a valuable insight on the power of selecting people in your social circle.

"Juggling an entrepreneurial career while trying to keep up with your grades, a social life and a relationship is no easy task. In my opinion, there's really no way out of making sacrifices to make it all happen, but there are some ways to make it easier on yourself.

I think the most helpful piece of advice I could provide college-student entrepreneurs would be to make a very conscious decision about the kind of people you spend time with. I found a group of friends who were all entrepreneurially minded and focused individuals. We studied together, launched a startup together and supported each other. This made it easier for me to still have a social life while simultaneously working on my entrepreneurial ventures.

Today, that same group of individuals continues to support me, and those relationships have helped me build my dream entrepreneurial career while continuing to travel the world with my girlfriend [now fiancée]."

The harsh reality is that you might have people in your world who will not be supportive of your startup; they might be naysayers or negative in general. These are not helpful people to spend time with when launching and growing your startup.

After the excitement of sharing your logo and your website, winning that startup pitch competition and telling your friends and family that you have a startup fades – when things get really tough – you need to have positive people who support you and your goal. You need people you can lean on when things are tough, in addition to people who are helpful to the startup. This might mean you have to stop spending time with some people who have been a regular part of your social life until now. This is not always easy.

As previously discussed, it is vital to get critical feedback from prospective customers and experts. You don't want to avoid these people just because you feel they are being negative because they might be providing insights that could make or break your startup. It's important to be able to extract the valuable feedback without getting defensive.

More likely than not, you won't have a significant amount of money when you start this project but you'll need help and guidance from others to make sure your startup is successful. This is when you seek out "advisors." Some of these people should be experts in the market (industry) that you are entering. Other advisors can help you with functional expertise such as sales, legal matters, accounting, software development, and more. These people need to understand they are *not* paid. You need to make that crystal clear. They are helping you because they believe in you and your startup, not to generate an income. Ask your professors, alumni, student organization leaders, startup accelerators, and incubators for recommendations of advisors who could help.

Eventually, you are going to have to build your startup team. You need to select people who have the skills that your startup needs. This is not a time to simply hire your roommate or your best friend. Spend time thinking about what your startup needs to get accomplished such as: Developing the mobile app, building a website, developing contracts, making sales calls, raising startup funds, etc. Then seek out the best people you can to help your startup while minimizing your costs.

Startup Insight: You will probably need to make some tough decisions about who you spend time with if you launch your startup. Surround yourself with positive, knowledgeable people who will support you, your startup and help you live a more productive and happier life.

Taking Control of Your Time

When you are in college, you are given more freedom than ever before – freedom to choose your classes and friends and how to spend your time. When launching your startup, it can be easy to put off things that don't seem important, like creating a Business Model Canvas (in Canvanizer.com) or talking to potential customers, so you can hang out with your friends.

Usually the conversation in your head goes something like this: "I did enough this week; I deserve to go out with friends. I'll work on the startup tomorrow." Then, tomorrow comes and the same thing happens and you continue to waste time and not make progress on your startup.

In order to provide yourself time to focus time on your startup, in addition to your classes and other activities, consider creating a time budget. It may seem ridiculous because you haven't had to do this before but, trust me, it works. First, block off the time that you sleep, then block the times that you need to commit to academics (classes, labs and group projects). Next, block off time for extracurriculars (such as startup-relevant clubs and student organizations like the Collegiate Entrepreneurs Organization.). After accounting for all of these, you should have roughly 60 hours left each week for going out, grabbing lunch with friends, watching Netflix and working on your startup. As you will soon find out, the time you spend going out, grabbing lunch with friends and watching Netflix will quickly turn into startup time!

Now is where the real work comes in. Start keeping track of how you're spending your time.

My former student, Austin Beveridge, consistently demonstrated ways to maximize his productive time. This allowed him to focus time on his girlfriend, classes and time (not always in that order).

Austin shared with me the method he used to budget his time.

"I used this method [below] when budgeting my time. I began by tracking how I was spending my time, much like counting calories or creating a budget.

- Monday:
    - Wake up: 8 a.m., breakfast: 8:30-9, class: 9-12, lunch: 12-1, class: 1-3, hanging out and homework: 3-5, dinner: 5-6, flag football: 6-8, startup: 8-9, Netflix 9-11, Bed.
- Friday:
    - Wake up: 9 a.m., breakfast: 10, hangout/lunch: 11-1, homework/study: 1-2, Netflix: 2-4, volleyball: 4-5, dinner: 5-6, startup: 6-7, Netflix: 7-9, go out: 9-2 a.m., Bed.

At the end of the week, tally up how much time you spent doing everything, just like this:

- Sleep: 60 hours
- Class: 30 hours
- Netflix: 25 hours
- Meals: 20 hours
- Studying: 15 hours
- Extracurricular Activities: 10 hours
- Startup: 8 hours

"Then I created an action plan to identify how you're going to change your schedule to make the most of your time. Here are some of the tips I would give to most people:"

- To "Create" More Time:
    - Wake up an hour earlier than normal each weekday, like 7 a.m.
    - Create a list of 2-3 goals you'd like to achieve each day.
    - Download an app (like Off-time or Moment) that tracks and limits time spent on social media.
    - Setup a timer on Netflix/Hulu that automatically turns it off after one hour.

- o Pick two nights each week to go out with your friends and stick to them.

- When Working:
  - o Focus on one project at a time. Knock it out and move on.
  - o Immediately address any task that will take less than 2 minutes to complete, make a note of any that will take longer and schedule time later in the day/week to address.
  - o Pause text message and social media notifications while working.
  - o Take frequent breaks (5 mins for every 25 mins working). Download an app that automatically notifies you when to start/stop, i.e., the Pomodoro Technique.
    - Check your phone for emails/texts during the breaks.

Now, let's look at some tools to help turn your personal productivity into action.

Tools to Maximize Your Personal Productivity

If you need to manage your to-dos for yourself, there are many software application options. Here is a 2019 review of some options to help manage your personal time from PC Magazine:

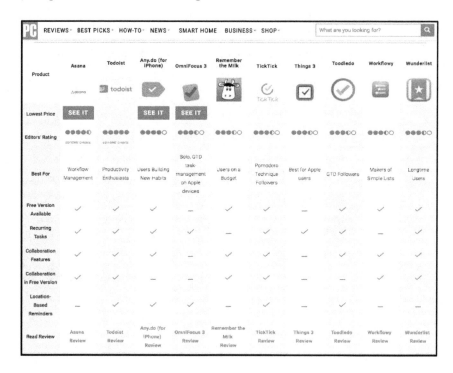

	Asana	Todoist	Any.do (for iPhone)	OmniFocus 3	Remember the Milk	TickTick	Things 3	Toodledo	Workflowy	Wunderlist
Product										
Lowest Price	SEE IT		SEE IT	SEE IT						
Editors' Rating	●●●●◐	●●●●●	●●●●◐	●●●●○	●●●◐○	●●●◐○	●●●◐○	●●●◐○	●●●◐○	●●●◐○
Best For	Workflow Management	Productivity Enthusiasts	Users Building New Habits	Solo, GTD task-management on Apple devices	Users on a Budget	Pomodoro Technique Followers	Best for Apple users	GTD Followers	Makers of Simple Lists	Longtime Users
Free Version Available	✓	✓	✓	—	✓	✓	—	✓	✓	✓
Recurring Tasks	✓	✓	✓	✓	—	✓	✓	✓	—	✓
Collaboration Features	✓	✓	✓	—	✓	✓	—	✓	✓	✓
Collaboration in Free Version	✓	✓	—	—	✓	✓	—	—	✓	✓
Location-Based Reminders	—	✓	✓	✓	—	✓	—	✓	—	—
Read Review	Asana Review	Todoist Review	Any.do (for iPhone) Review	OmniFocus 3 Review	Remember the Milk Review	TickTick Review	Things 3 Review	Toodledo Review	Workflowy Review	Wunderlist Review

Tools to Manage Your Startup's Productivity

You will find that using messaging apps, texting or sending emails is an incredibly inefficient way to communicate with your team and manage work.

However, there are fantastic tools, some of which are free, to help drive you and your team to maximize your startup's growth. Some focus on communications and others on project management. Some can do both.

Here are some of the most common tools used for communications and project management:

1. Asana – Communications tool with project due date functionality.
2. Basecamp – Project management with To-Do lists and discussions.
3. Microsoft SharePoint – Connects and communicates with all Microsoft Office products.
4. Trello – To-do list functionality with online whiteboard functionality.
5. Slack – Communications tool with file storage. Connects to a multitude of other applications.

Slack is currently considered the "gold standard" in the startup world. I use it in my startups and even require my students to use it in my classes when they are developing startup ideas and other group projects. Slack effectively eliminates the need for email, texting and direct messaging. Slack has an easy-to-use UI (user interface) and a clean mobile app version. Slack even provides a free version that includes all the functionality that most startups need.

Slack

The last important thing to mention is the shift in mindset that needs to take place when you are in college and simultaneously launching your startup.

The Entrepreneurial Roller Coaster

You will probably never experience such emotional highs and lows in your life as those you'll experience as an entrepreneur. You will feel like you are riding an out-of-control roller coaster at times. Hang on to the excitement when someone tells you, "I would definitely pay for that," "You need to build that," "That would really help our business grow," "That would save us so much time," "You would cut our costs by 40 percent," and "You have to do this!" Those times of excitement help you through the roller coaster valleys when people are telling you, "Your product sucks," "You charge too much," "I don't have the money to pay you." You may even have to fire one of your first employees or decide your co-founder should leave the startup. By the way, I have personally experienced all of these. You just have to get back on and continue the ride.

I had a conversation with my dear friend and mentor Joe Jeka one day, a few months after I launched Sales Sherpas, my first startup. Frankly, I was whining a little bit about the lack of appreciation customers were showing for how hard I was working to make them happy. I was returning emails late into the evening, answering my cell phone whenever they called, delivering the marketing campaigns early, producing great sales results, and still, rarely did they bestow compliments for my hard work.

Joe listened quietly and then responded firmly, "*Dave, they thank you every time they pay you!*"

We are used to receiving praise and thanks in life. When you have a startup in college, you need to shift your mindset from being rewarded for good work with good grades and praise from your professors, to the ping of your smartphone notifying you that an electronic payment was just submitted to your bank account.

When you sit back and think, "I created a product or service, from nothing, that is improving the lives of people so much that they are willing to pay me," it is a much more powerful feeling than any grade you will receive.

STEP
04

Finding Helpful Resources for Your Startup

Step 4 – Locating Helpful Resources
For Your College Startup

Contrary to Sun Tzu's "Burn the bridges" quote from 2,500 years ago, when it comes to the world of startups, burning metaphorical bridges is an awful idea. As a side note: If you haven't read *The Art of War*, grab a copy and be prepared to learn great lessons on analyzing your market, building your team, motivating your team, and leading your team to success. I used this book in my MBA courses at the University of Wisconsin-Madison and it was very well received.

I have seen college-student entrepreneurs, telling their professors (both indirectly and directly) that their startup is a priority over their classes. This is definitely a way to burn your bridges.

As Henry Schwartz referenced in the previous chapter, you can actually use your classes to complement your startup, help other students learn, and get better grades than students without a startup.

You are experiencing college at one of the most exciting times in history! Never before has there been as much money and time dedicated to the world of entrepreneurship by colleges and universities.

Helpful resources available to college-student entrepreneurs include:

1. More entrepreneurship college courses than ever before (including online).
2. Adoption of entrepreneurship majors and minors throughout the world.
3. Increased number of pitch competitions.
4. Increased number of grants.
5. Alumni interested in funding startups.

6. Crowdfunding services such as Kickstarter, Indiegogo and GoFundMe.
7. Legal entrepreneurship clinics that provide free legal support.
8. Lower legal status filing fees.
9. Startup accelerator programs both inside and outside of colleges.
10. Free office space.
11. College credits for launching your startup.
12. More experienced startup mentors available at college and externally.
13. Entrepreneurship conferences at the local, state and national level.
14. Low-cost and free web-based services (e.g., eLance, Slack, Google Drive).
15. Special academic accommodations from some professors.

I spoke with Sam Lepak, another one of my former, very creative, and innovative student entrepreneurs.

Sam Lepak launched two startups before graduation. One startup, named Intern Betas, provided internships for students seeking experience with startups. His second startup, Pintful Peanut Butter, provided a high energy, all-natural peanut butter. While at college, he worked at gener8tor, one of the fastest growing startup accelerators in the U.S. He next led digital marketing for Yacht Life. Next, Sam went on to launch his own digital marketing business. He is now, literally, touring the world while managing social marketing campaign strategies for clients.

I interviewed Sam to help students understand how to leverage the college student experience as a way to accelerate the launch of a startup.

"College is what you make of it. Plain and simple. The opportunities that you have to develop a startup business, refine it and launch while at college are limitless!

Some students find out what excites them and start building the business of their dreams (if that's what excites them), while others squander the period of time and wish they had been more focused. If building a business to solve a problem is what excites you, then you're at an ideal point to do it. Don't wait … the only thing stopping you is YOU!

As a college student, you are almost automatically handed a virtual "cute student card" that allows you to ask for help from practically everyone. Use this card to your advantage. The card is used for asking for advice on all aspects of building a business – pitfalls to avoid, product development and traction strategies, and much more. For example, if you are conducting research on a startup idea, simply explain to the target person, "I am a university student from XYZ university and am conducting research on a startup idea. Would you be willing to meet to share your insights for 20-30 minutes? I have literally spoken to hundreds of people who have helped me refine startup ideas and launch new products and services. I never could have done any of it if I hadn't taken advantage of the opportunity of being a student."

Entrepreneurship Courses

Many entrepreneurship courses are now available to you. Even if your college does not offer these courses, you can take them online through other colleges or universities.

Here are examples of some of the more common college entrepreneurship courses from the University of Wisconsin-Whitewater Entrepreneurship Program.

1. Introduction to Entrepreneurship
2. New Business Feasibility
3. Entrepreneurial Finance
4. Entrepreneurial Marketing
5. Entrepreneurial Law
6. Social Entrepreneurship
7. Family Entrepreneurship
8. Growing Entrepreneurial Organizations
9. Strategic Entrepreneurship

If you are going to invest time and money to take these courses, I highly recommend you locate courses taught by instructors who have had their own startups. These instructors will provide invaluable, pragmatic insights you will otherwise not receive from someone who doesn't possess the real-world startup experience. Before you sign up for a class, research the instructor on LinkedIn to see if they have startup experience that can help you.

Pitch Competitions

Pitch competitions provide college entrepreneurs the tremendous opportunity to not only raise capital to help fund their startup but also opportunities to refine their business model. Frequently, the best insights will come from judges who are angel investors and venture capitalists. These individuals have seen a great deal of startups and the most successful ones will have developed a formula for success. They will share these insights with you in the form of their questions, notes from their judging sheets (if they make these available) and feedback they will likely provide you after the event, if you ask. If you do not network with these judges after the event, you are missing a significant opportunity to learn insights from them and help grow your startup.

There are some pitfalls with pitch competitions that need to be avoided. I have seen many students put so much energy into these competitions that they lose focus on refining their business model, launching, and growing their startups. I also find that students have unrealistic expectations about the amount of money they will raise from the competitions. Many of these events have a significant number of applicants and, unfortunately, the available prize money can be very low. Personally, I think it's a terrible disservice when the organizations that manage pitch competitions are not upfront about the application requirements, the number of stages in the competition, or the prizes that can be won.

Regardless, I do recommend that all students experience at least one pitch competition. The experience is invaluable and an effective process can be to apply to a local or university-sponsored competition before moving up to a statewide, regional or national competition. For example, at the University of

Wisconsin-Whitewater, we have students apply for our Elevator Pitch Competition and Warhawk Business Plan Competition and then move on to the Wisconsin Big Idea Competition, Wisconsin Governor's Business Plan Competition, Future Founders Competition the Collegiate Entrepreneurs Organization Global Conference Competition or TCU's Values and Ventures Competition.

If you decide you would like to apply to a pitch competition, there are practical insights to help you in Step 8: Pitching Your Startup.

Law Clinics

Historically, one of the major barriers to entry for startups has been legal costs. The process of applying for legal status at the state level was incredibly laborious and costly, However, this is starting to change. Some states, such as Wisconsin, have lowered the LLC filing fee from $130 to free for college students. We are not recommending that all startups apply for an LLC. See Step 6: Law School For Your Startup for details.

Many universities with law schools are now offering law and entrepreneurship clinics. These clinics typically provide free or discounted legal services. Typically, these clinics are managed by law professors and/or practicing attorneys. The actual work is frequently done by law school students. The benefit for the law school is that it can provide students an opportunity to practice their craft on nascent businesses. The benefit for entrepreneurs is that they receive low-cost/no-cost services.

Here are some examples of the services offered by the University of Wisconsin Law and Entrepreneurship Clinic:

- Entity selection and registration
- State and local business licenses
- Federal, state and local tax issues
- Financing documents
- Leases and other commercial contracts
- Employment agreements

- Trademark and copyright registration
- Provisional patent applications and licensing agreements
- Intellectual property counseling regarding branding, copyrights, trademarks, trade secrets, freedom to operate, unfair competition, antitrust, publicity rights and privacy rights

Law and Entrepreneurship Clinics will typically have an application process that needs to be followed in order to ensure that the law clinic can provide the help requested and that the applicant's needs will provide a valuable experience for the law school students.

Here are some examples, from the Marquette Law and Entrepreneurship Clinic:

1. What products or services does your business offer?
2. Have you formed a legal entity yet?
3. Describe the past activities and milestones for your business.
4. Describe what you hope to accomplish in the next 6-12 months.
5. What is the target market for your product or service?
6. Describe how your business will create jobs.
7. How do you plan to fund your business?
8. How much time do the founders/owners of the business plan devote to it?
9. Describe all the legal services you believe your business currently needs.
10. What is your timing for the legal services?

Final considerations with law and entrepreneurship clinics

Just because you apply for legal services at a law and entrepreneurship clinic, that doesn't mean they will provide the legal services. I don't let my startups or student startups apply without a complete business plan detailing the products and services, team, marketing and sales plan and financial forecasts. If you are not willing to put in this work, why should they put work into your startup?

Keep in mind that most of the work will be done by law school students, but they are typically supervised by law school professors or attorneys working in a law practice.

Lastly, in most law schools, the only grades that law school students receive is on their end of semester exam. So, guess when you shouldn't expect a rapid turnaround on the work? Yes, that's right, at the end of the semester. I always recommend my students apply at the end of a previous semester or right away at the beginning of a semester. This gives the law school students plenty of time to do the work.

Startup Accelerators

Startup accelerators provide short-term programs to help startups test or refine their business model. These programs can help dramatically increase the success of entrepreneurs and their startups.

Some progressive colleges already have successful startup accelerators in place. Stanford's Startup X program is one such model program.

You can see some of the benefits of student startup accelerators below:

1. Training
2. Mentoring
3. Weekly roundtables
4. Business model development
5. Free office space
6. Free Wi-Fi
7. Legal connections
8. Accounting connections
9. Software development
10. Pitch competition preparation
11. Pitch deck preparation
12. Startup capital

I would be remiss if I didn't mention something about receiving startup capital from colleges. Most colleges that provide startup funding will do so as a "grant."

Note: This is no different from a scholarship grant you might have received. There is nothing to pay back, obviously, unless you drop out of college or transfer to a different college. I am painfully aware of "grants losses" when transferring schools because my daughter transferred to a college with a better program for her field of study. Losing money is never fun.

Some colleges will provide startup capital but seek equity in the student's startup in exchange for the funding. Be careful that you understand whether you are receiving a grant or giving up equity. There are significant implications of giving up equity too early in the life of your startup. I will save that insight for the next book.

Incubators

Launching and managing your startup can be accomplished with your own passion, intelligence, creativity, intestinal fortitude and, yes, a laptop in your dorm room.

However, there is a significant benefit to having a dedicated space to go and work on your startup. When I began my first startup, it was at my home. Although it helped save a great deal of money, I could never "turn it off." I found that having a dedicated place to go to work (that wasn't in my home) helped me focus when I was there and avoid the distractions at home - or, in your case, your dorm room or apartment. So, having an office space can help reduce your stress.

Secondly, office space in places like startup incubators (buildings dedicated to startups and growing firms) provides opportunities for camaraderie with other entrepreneurs. It is going to be tough for your roommate, who has no interest in your startup, to provide insights and motivation to help launch and grow your idea. Whereas, at an incubator, you will likely be surrounded by entrepreneurs who will provide you emotional support and strategies to help your startup grow.

Startup incubators can also serve as fantastic opportunities to network with not only other entrepreneurs but angel investors, startup mentors, software engineers, attorneys and obviously other entrepreneurs.

Lastly, incubators frequently provide helpful speakers, training programs and meet-ups to accelerate your personal as well as professional growth.

Incubators located in metropolitan areas, such as the award-winning 1871 in Chicago, are the home to startups, law firms, startup accelerators, special programs, large events and sometimes funding. These full-service incubators tend to be more expensive, provide less personal and dedicated office space with monthly rents starting at $300+/month. However, many incubators will provide discounted rates for college students or even provide free office space, like our Whitewater Incubation Center.

Internships

You might be asking, "why are we talking about internships if I am looking at starting my own business?" It probably goes without saying that you will learn more by going through the process of launching your own startup versus having a traditional internship. However, if you carefully think through the market in which your startup operates, for example transportation, an internship at a large transportation company might make sense. You can gather deep industry experience in a specific functional area but ideally you will get exposure to many functional areas. For example: You might dive into marketing, finance, software development, recruiting all within one internship.

Typically, internships with large companies will be focused on one specific facet of a company and require a long-term commitment (typically months). For example, you might spend months attending meetings where topics include areas that will not help drive your startup idea forward. You might be making a very good income but the opportunity-cost of your time is significant. Specifically, I am referring to the value of your time and what else you could be doing with your time. There are exceptions, which I will discuss in a minute.

So, when we look at internships versus spending the time on your startup, consider the following: How much is my time worth and what is the total cost of taking an internship vs. spending the time on my startup?

You might say, "Well my time is worth $15/hour and they are paying me $15/hour and so this internship makes sense." But what you are not considering is the opportunity-cost of not working on your startup. Time spent on the internship is time that can be lost working on your startup. If you want to get the pilot/beta for your startup launched and the internship is a full-time internship for three months, then you might not want to take the internship. You might say, "But I need the money." This is definitely a consideration, but I would challenge you to think of other ways to acquire that money. What about crowdfunding your startup through Kickstarter or getting loans or an investment from parents? Note, Step #7 covers funding your startup in depth.

Here is a final consideration, and this is very important. There are new models for internships that can be short-term and project based and you can be highly selective. An example of project-based internships can be found at a new firm called Got Interns.

I interviewed Jeff Peterson, who is the CEO and Co-Founder of Geneva Supply and brainchild behind Got Interns. Geneva Supply was ranked #29 out of 360 startups by Entrepreneur Magazine. Their ranking is based on four metrics: impact, innovation, growth and leadership (source: Entrepreneur.com). Geneva Supply's core business is managing logistics and marketing on Amazon and other eCommerce platforms. In addition to Geneva Supply, Jeff launched a program called Biz Tank for high school students and BizHub for college students. Both of these programs provide powerful work experiences that are relevant to students' areas of interests in an effort to help them navigate their future or current careers. This work led Jeff to the launch Got Interns.

Here is a part of my interview with Jeff:

"I launched Got Interns with my team. It's essentially the match.com between college students seeking practical, real-world experience that is relevant to their desired career. We also didn't want to tie students down to internships that lasted months but didn't provide valuable knowledge or insights that would really help them out. For example, if a student is a marketing major, we might have them work on a digital marketing campaign for a client that utilizes Amazon. The digital marketing campaign might only require 20 hours of work and need to be completed in four weeks. We also are passionate about helping college students who want to launch their own startups. So, if a student tells us they want to launch their own company, we will provide an internship with a startup or early stage company. Another example might be that a student entrepreneur needs experience developing a mobile app, so we might match them with a mobile app development company. Got Interns is only focused on internships that will help college students and accelerate them toward their desired careers or successfully launch their startup!"

Special Accommodations

This is the portion of the book you should NOT share with your college professors. Shhhhhhhh.

As we discussed earlier in the book, many student entrepreneurs are now receiving some of the perks that historically have been reserved for student athletes!

Here are some tips on asking for special accommodations to attend startup events such as a pitch competition or entrepreneur's conference:

1. Always be respectful of your professor.
   - Provide advanced notice (ideally at the beginning of the semester).
   - Don't ask them, "Will there be anything important that we will be covering?" You are in essence saying, will you be wasting my time again? Not a good idea.

2. Get help
   - It is always best to get another instructor, a faculty advisor who is assisting you, to write the email. They will almost always have more influence on a positive outcome than you will.
3. Get it in writing.
   - Don't leave a voicemail.
   - If you are attending the event by yourself, write a professional email including the reason for the special accommodation, the educational value of the event/experience, your name, student ID number, preferred email address and phone number.

Example: Requesting an Excused Absence Letter

Dear Professor Gee,

I am truly enjoying your Introduction to Entrepreneurship - 201 class. I would like to ask permission to miss your class on Tuesday, November 1st and Thursday, November 3rd and not receive any point deductions because of a conference I will be attending. I realize I will be responsible for all of the content you provide and assignments that are due on those dates or assigned on those dates.

I will be attending the Collegiate Entrepreneurs Organization (CEO) National Conference in Kansas City. During this conference, I will be participating in the CEO National Pitch Competition, learning from world-class entrepreneur presentations, participating in entrepreneur workshops, networking with other entrepreneurs and learning about finance for small businesses through conversations with angel investors.

Could you please let me know by October 1st if I will not receive the point deduction?

Thank you for your consideration.

Sam Lepak

Startup Insight: Some professors will provide you special accommodations for you and your startup. Special accommodations can include: no point deductions for missing classes, extra credit for participating in pitch competitions and opportunities to share your startup idea in your classes to get student feedback.

Step 5 – Branding and Marketing Your Startup

What is a brand?

First, let's talk about what a brand is. I am sure you have heard many different definitions. The one I feel most efficiently and effectively captures the essence of a brand is the following: A brand is a promise of the value a company, product or service will provide to their customers. The brand is how you represent your customer value proposition.

Within the area of marketing, developing your brand can be one of the most enjoyable, but also one of the most maddening processes. It is critical to take the time to consider your brand through your customer's eyes first, and not your own. Use words that make it clear what your product or service provides. You might have brand names for various products and services. For now, we are going to focus on creating a brand name for your startup itself.

Sexy vs. Specific Scale

I have found that entrepreneurs usually gravitate toward creating a brand name that is sexy, exciting and one they "perceive" to be memorable. When I am meeting with entrepreneurs to discuss development of their brand names, I grab my dry erase marker, head to the whiteboard and write the following;

Avoid the Brand Name Boat Anchor

The temptation when created the brand name for your startup idea is to create some **"Sexy."** However, when you marketing budget is small or $0 you don't have the luxury of brand that is sexy. Instead you need to quickly convey what your brand is and the product/service of the brand. If you don't your brand is going to get lost in the hundreds or thousands of other brands that people see every day. You need to focus on **"Specific"** and not "Sexy." Now, there are exceptions to this rule, for example, if your brand is complimenting other products that you own, you can quickly explain the product in a tagline or other value proposition, etc.

One of the main considerations I see entrepreneurs overlooking is the impact their brand name has on search engine optimization (SEO). SEO is the proactive process you go through in an effort to increase your page rank utilizing organic or "free" methods (not paid advertisements). Page rank is the position a website occupies on a search engine (e.g. Second place down on a search within Google) relative to other websites. Think about the specific words (aka keywords) customers will type into a search engine if they are looking for a product/service such as yours.

For example, if we type "hats" in the search box within Google, the screen shown in the graphic below pops up. Notice that the third actual search result (not paid ads—the images on top and the first search result "Lids") is for hats.com. That is about the least sexy brand name you can imagine. But you will notice they are on the first page of Google. In fact, they appear within the first three spots (which is important) ... without spending any money. I am not saying you should not spend money on paid search advertising; it can be very cost-effective. But, why spend money you don't have just to increase your visibility in search engines when you could be spending that money in other ways to launch and grow your startup?

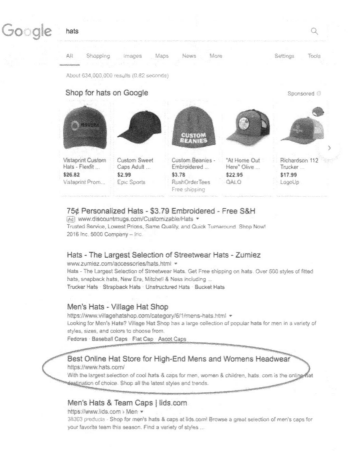

So, throw out sexy brand names. They will serve as your page rank boat anchor. Instead, move on to names that will help you gain customer recognition, and save your marketing dollars for driving sales, not making you feel good.

When choosing a name, the best place to start is by defining your target market and defining the benefits you will provide. That name then represents your value proposition.

Startup Insight: When developing your startup brand name, avoid the temptation to create a sexy name that does not communicate a clear message to your customer about what you do, especially since that name can simultaneously hurt your page rank.

Brand Name Creation in Action

As mentioned earlier, we will use a fictional company as an example as we move through the process of creating a brand. I have intentionally created a service that is easy to understand and won't distract you from the process of creating your brand name.

This startup is focused on helping provide software to in-home providers of support for senior citizens.

Customer Segments	Benefits Provided
Homebound seniors	Safety, Time Savings, Convenience, Savings
Children of homebound seniors	Peace-of-mind, Convenience, Financial Savings
Visiting nurses	Convenience, Time Savings
Physicians	Convenience, Time Savings

Now we have identified the customer segments and benefits for each customer segment. In this case, "convenience" is a universal benefit. There might be a benefit to the primary customer, in this case, homebound seniors, that overrides all of the other benefits (e.g. safety of the homebound senior person).

A sound strategy is to combine your customer segment(s) with the benefit(s). This is a great time to use a website such as thesaurus.com to search for synonyms.

To continue with the example, let's select the word "senior" to represent our customer segment. Next, we decide that "convenience" is too vague, so we select "aid" instead.

In this case, let's create the brand name "Senior Aid."

Trademark Implications

Before moving on with selecting your brand name, you should search the United States Patent and Trademark Office website to ensure your brand name is not taken, so you can avoid trademark infringement. Simply go to: uspto.gov. Consult your attorney for additional insights into using a trademark name if someone is already using the one you've chosen. You might find another company is using the name, but for a different product with a different target market. This could have very different implications than if a company is using the same name and targeting the same or similar customers.

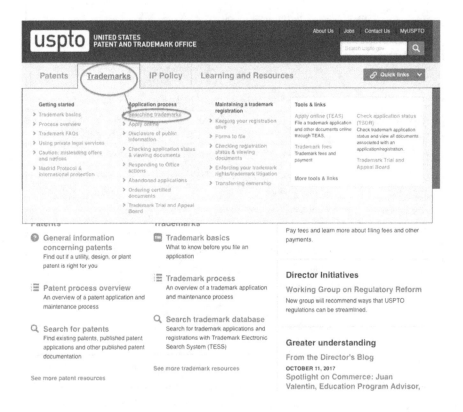

You do not have to pay to register your trademark, but it is safest to do so. Trademarking the name gives you the most legal protection. Once you receive the trademark approval, begin putting the ® next to your brand name. However, many startups will simply put the "TM" next to their name if they are selling a product and "SM" if they selling a service. Using ™ or SM is basically a way of saying, "if you use our brand, we will file a complaint with the USPTO for using our brand name." However, in order to file a complaint, that company name must first be registered. As of the writing of this book, the cost to file for a trademark with the USPTO is $275. Obviously, you can pay your attorney to do it for you if you so choose.

There are more details to follow on trademarks in "Step 6 - Law School for Your Startup."

Selecting your Website Address

Your website address, also known as a URL (universal resource locator), is critically important to most startup companies. It is one of the most efficient and effective ways to market your business. You need to take a scientific approach to selecting your website address, because it will determine the amount of traffic you attract to your website, landing page, social media sites, etc. I see so many entrepreneurs just selecting something sexy that has no clear expression of what the company does. Sometimes they will select a website address that doesn't even match the brand name they have created. If you have $5 million to promote your brand, then ignore this section. If you don't, pay attention—website address class is now in session.

First, check the availability on a website address service provider such as GoDaddy. There are less expensive services than them, but GoDaddy provides website addresses, website builder software, integrated payment services, hosting, email addresses and more.

Returning to our fictional company, Senior Aid, we want to select a name for our website that is the same as our brand name. We will also need to consider the domain extension (e.g. .com, .net, .org). In general, it's best to check for a .com domain first. It is the most commonly used domain extension for businesses.

So, let's go to GoDaddy and type "senioraid.com" in the domain search field. You can see the results below.

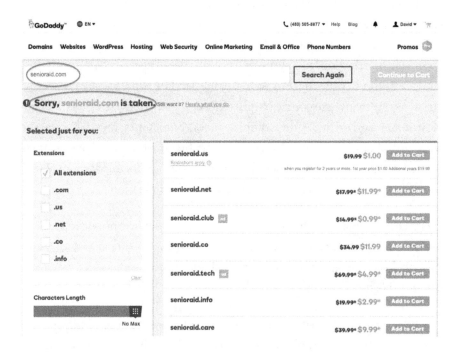

Unfortunately, in this case, senioraid.com is taken. Determining that someone has already purchased a website address that matches our brand can be a very deflating experience for entrepreneurs. However, all is not lost!

At this point we have three primary options:

1. Change the name of the website address we want to use (and also change our brand name).
2. Locate the owner of the website address and try to purchase it from them.
3. Select a website address with a different domain extension.

If you have spent a great deal of time creating your brand and have received positive feedback from prospective customers, stick with your brand and proceed to one of the last two options.

First, let's see if there is an active website tied to the website address that we want to use. I typed "senioraid.com" into the address bar of the browser and this little gem popped-up. The good news is the website address is probably not being used. The bad news is that we don't know who to contact to purchase the website address.

Actually, there is more good news. There are web-based tools whereby you can locate the owner of a domain name. Let the detective work begin. I simply went to "ICANN Who Is" and typed in senioraid.com into the Lookup text box.

This is what popped up:

We have discovered there is a private owner of the website address. You will notice there is a phone number. Frequently, there is an email address and phone number of the "Registrant Contact," but unfortunately, in this case, we just have a phone number. So, I made the call to the phone number listed and got no answer. I can choose to keep calling or select another domain extension.

I do need to give you a heads-up on something that creates a great deal of pain for those legitimately seeking website addresses for their businesses. There are companies around the world that aggregate website addresses and resell them; they are sometimes known as domain squatters. We won't get into a discussion about how I feel about these companies, but given that one of my greatest passions is helping budding entrepreneurs, you can probably imagine. These companies purchase URLs they think will be popular in the future and then turnaround and sell these website addresses, frequently for prices that first-time entrepreneurs can't afford.

I had a friend that launched a tech startup (with which you are all familiar) in San Francisco, that experienced explosive growth. Unfortunately, I cannot share their name. They were absolutely set on their brand name, as were their investors who had invested tens of millions of dollars into the company. The website address holder found out who the startup was, and the good old rule of supply and demand kicked in. The squatter would not release the website address for less than $50k. His startup actually paid the $50k. Before you start feeling sorry for him, you should know that he ended up selling his company for over $150 million.

I am not advocating you pay exorbitant prices for website addresses, especially when you are in startup mode and every dollar is precious. In fact, I recommend quite the opposite. Here is a strategy to deal with situations when you cannot locate a potential seller of a website address or when they are asking an astronomical price that just isn't practical for your startup.

You instead could use another domain type such as .us, .net (which represents Internet service providers), or .org (which represents nonprofits). Note: When we say nonprofits, we are not referring to startups that don't make a profit but, rather, organizations that are specifically not-for-profit such as charities.

One strategy used by startups now, based on the number of .com website addresses that have been taken, is utilizing .io. The origin of .io is that it represents "Indian Ocean." However, many tech firms will just say it represents "Input Output."

Back to our Senior Aid example...

So, we search for senioraid.io. Voila! Senioraid.io is available. Next, we simply pay for the website address. We can also add email connected to the website address. For example, if your name is Bob, you might select: bob@senioraid.io.

Social Media Addresses

The next thing we want to do is check social media website address availability. There are services such as "KnowEm" (knowem.com) that allow you to easily check availability of all the major social media service providers.

To continue with our example of Senior Aid, we will now check the availability of "senioraid" on the major social media services using knowem.com. In this case, the graphic below shows our results. We can see social media services such as YouTube and Facebook are available, but many others are unavailable. It is rarely a good idea to not select a startup brand name just because it lacks availability on social media. However, if you are a B2C brand, and you have discovered that your target market is going to primarily locate you through a specific media service or services, then you might decide to choose another brand name.

Creating Your Logo

Once we have created our brand name, purchased our website address and checked availability on social media addresses, we can move on to creating our logo. This part can be really fun (no sarcasm intended).

This is not one of those times to rely on your nephew who is a graphic designer taking a "gap year" to work as a ski lift operator in Vail™. There are much more rapid ways to get logo designs created. I recommend sources such as Fiverr fiverr.com or Elance elance.com. It is important to provide as much "artistic direction" as possible when asking for a design.

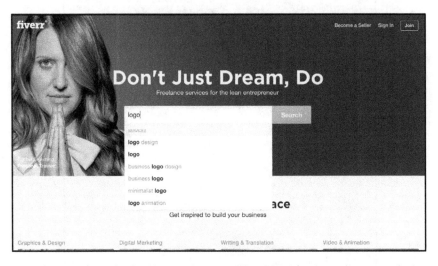

Provide samples of other logos that you like. Provide the colors you desire. Interestingly, colors used on websites follow trends. I recommend conducting a search for the most popular colors if you are launching a business-to-consumer brand.

Choosing the Colors for your Brand

It is easy to just tell a graphic designer something like, "I like red and black—let's just go with that." However, we should consider the impact on consumer behavior.

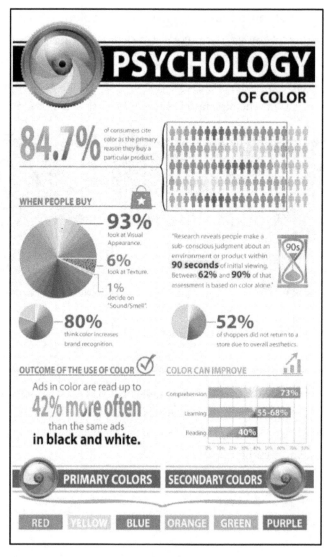

Source: *Fast Company, Psychology of Color (U.S.) Rachel Gillett, 3/13/14*

Below is a chart based on color popularity of websites in 2016.

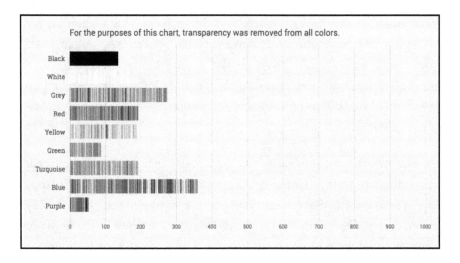

Source: Wired Magazine, Margaret Rhodes, 9/13/16

There are considerations of emotion that are created by colors, which should be considered when creating your logo.

Some of the recurring themes are:

- Yellow connotes optimism.
- Orange connotes friendliness.
- Blue connotes trust and dependability.
- Red connotes excitement and power.
- Purple connotes creativity.
- Green connotes peacefulness.
- Gray connotes balance.

Source: Entrepreneur Magazine, 4/13/2017

Providing Artistic Direction

Some entrepreneurs find the process of deciding on a logo laborious and frustrating. They complain about how the graphic designer is "not creative," "they don't understand," "they are not getting it," etc. Typically, these problems result from not providing the graphic designer enough "artistic direction." Artistic direction, in this context, refers to providing graphic design guidance.

For example, you might request that a graphic designer incorporates blue and white, the Arial font and an image that represents teamwork. Some graphic designers might get defensive, saying you are not providing them enough artistic license. Designers can be a sensitive bunch at times. Heap praise on them, but hold them to timelines. It is easy to waste exorbitant amounts of time creating a logo Don't fall into this trap. Remember, your goal is to get your startup beta/pilot rolling, satisfy customers and validate your business model as soon as you can. You can always modify or change your logo later.

Marketing Your Startup

Marketing 101

Here is a crash course in marketing if you are a non-marketer. One of the mistakes a non-marketer often makes is automatically thinking that marketing is only advertising. Marketing is much more than that, and understanding this is critical for the startup founder.

The classic definition of the marketing mix, also known as the "4Ps," is comprised, as you probably guessed, of four elements:

1. Product
2. Place
3. Price
4. Promotion

This is where the academics will chime in and yell, "Gee, you missed the 7Ps and 8Ps." Fair point. The "7Ps" represent an additional three elements of process, people and physical evidence and the "8Ps" will add "performance" to the "7Ps." For the sake of brevity, we are going to focus on the classic "4Ps."

Here is a graphic that details the "4Ps."

Marketing Mix (4 P's)

Product
- Functionality
- Brand
- Packaging
- Services

Price
- List Price
- Discounts
- Bundling
- Credit Terms

Target Market

Promotion
- Advertising
- Sales Force
- Publicity
- Sales Promotion

Place
- Channel
- Inventory
- Logistics
- Distribution

Marketing Plan Preparation

One of the temptations first-time entrepreneurs face is diving right into the fun stuff—the advertising of their startup—before they have even created a validated business model. If you have validated your business model already and have selected your brand name, it is now time to move on to marketing.

Marketing is the representation of your new life, and you want to share it with the world, so why not? If you arrived at this step and have not achieved validation, please go back and validate your concept. I have seen too many entrepreneurs throw all of their energy into the marketing of a startup idea when they should have spent it on validation. Many of those have resulted in a spectacular PUBLIC failure. Needless to say, this is not only bad for the startup itself, but it also damages the credibility of the entrepreneur.

If you have ensured you are personally ready, have conducted discovery, prepared your family, created your Business Model Canvas and developed your brand, it is now time to move on to developing your marketing plan.

We are going to create a very basic startup marketing plan for now.

Here are the critical elements for your marketing plan:

1. Define your target market(s).
2. Create your value proposition.
3. Develop your pricing.
4. Build your sales channels.
5. Identify your distribution channels.
6. Create your advertising.
7. Develop your marketing calendar.

Note: Many marketing plans include a comprehensive competitive analysis, which we did not create for the Senior Aid example.

Let's revisit Startup Aid and create a sample marketing plan.

Senior Aid Marketing Plan

Customer Value Proposition

Senior Aid provides a software solution to help manage and communicate services provided to seniors who receive in-home care, in an effort to increase safety and convenience, and provide peace of mind.

Customer segments:	Benefits provided:
Homebound seniors	Safety, Time Savings, Convenience, Cost Savings
Children of homebound seniors	Peace-of-mind, Convenience, Cost Savings
Visiting nurses	Convenience, Time Savings
Physicians	Convenience, Time Savings

Priority Markets

Senior Aid's market priorities will be as follows, based on market opportunity combined with market need:

1. Homebound seniors
2. Visiting nurses (organizations)
3. Physicians (clinics, hospitals, groups)

Senior Aid Services

1. Web-based software application
2. Administrative portal for the senior in-home care management company
3. Individual health service provider portal (to homebound seniors)
4. Family web portal (log-in)
5. Mobile application
6. Family portal
7. Family support provider referral program
8. Family support provider application
9. Family support provider selection process

10. Family support provider payment system to Senior Aid
11. Integrated payment system

1) Website

The Senior Aid website will be the hub of the sales channels' efforts. This will include access for healthcare service providers, families and physicians. We need to spend the time and financial resources to optimize the website for search engine optimization. At launch, we also should activate a paid search campaign on Google AdWords to drive initial traffic. Lastly, we should secure a banner ad on the AARP website (and link to an AARP-specific landing page on our website). We should rapidly secure testimonial videos from family members and seniors and incorporate them into our website's home page.

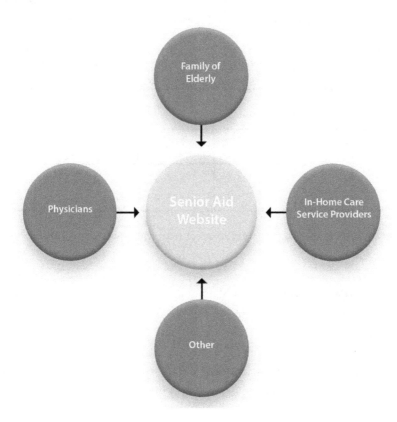

Logo

The Senior Aid logo will utilize blue and white in an effort to represent honesty and integrity. The shapes within the logo will represent the unification of family, the service provider and the seniors through the support provided by Senior Aid. A square version of the logo should also be created so it can be effectively incorporated into social media.

Marketing Messaging

Senior Aid has various audiences with different needs. It is critical that all audiences are considered in marketing efforts. Below are the primary audiences, their needs and the related messages we need to convey.

	Safety	Peace-of-Mind	Convenience	Time Savings	Profitability
Family	X	X	X		
Physicians			X	X	
Service Providers			X	X	X

Note: Marketing campaigns need to accentuate the messages relative to each audience.

Family marketing messaging: Marketing campaigns targeting the families of the seniors receiving in-home care should focus on safety, peace-of-mind and convenience.

Physicians marketing messaging: Marketing campaigns that target physicians should focus on convenience and time savings.

Service provider marketing messaging: Marketing campaigns targeting service providers should deliver a message that focuses on convenience, time savings and profitability.

Senior Aid Pricing

Our initial pricing model is below. Senior Aid will focus on the Basic and Plus plans during their beta phase.

	Basic	Plus	Pro	Elite
Senior Aid Basic Platform	✔	✔	✔	✔
One Family Portal	✔	✔	✔	✔
Up to 5 Family Portal log-ins	✔	✔	✔	✔
One Admin Portal log-in	✔	✔	✔	✔
Up to 5 Admin Portal log-ins	-	✔	✔	✔
Up to 20 Admin Portal log-ins	-	-	✔	✔
Private Webinar Training	-	-	-	✔
Phone Support per Month	-	Up to 30 minutes	Up to 1 hour	Up to 2 hours
Email Support per Month	1	1	Up to 5	Up to 10
In-Home Setup Sessions	0	0	0	Up to 20
Mobile App	-	✔	✔	✔
Portal Customization	-	-	-	-
Monthly Billing	-	-	-	✔
Annual Prepaid Billing	✔	✔	✔	-
Monthly Price	$99	$199	$299	$499

Promotion:

Most first-time entrepreneurs jump straight to the "promotion" element of the 4Ps and focus on advertising without considering pricing. The following methodology will describe how you can prioritize the market based on impact. Each of these marketing methodologies is listed in chronological order based on priority. The priority is based on efficiency and effectiveness. This means you should use methods that deliver the highest sales impact first. For our example, this would include methods that secure the newest service provider sign-ups for the lowest cost and minimal time commitment. With additional financial resources (e.g. from revenue and external investment) and additional labor (e.g. hiring of business development managers and marketers), we can become more aggressive.

Below is a matrix of the target markets with the associated marketing methodology:

	Senior Aid Website	Business Development (Emails, webinars, sales calls)	Paid Search Advertising	Trade shows	Public Relations and Social Media
Service Providers	1	2	5	4	3
Families	1	N/A	2	N/A	3
Physicians	1	5	N/A	N/A	2

2) Business Development (Sales) Efforts

As do most software firms targeting an SMB (small- and medium-sized business) market, we will focus on the most efficient ways to secure a high volume of customers. This will involve marketing efforts focused on driving prospective service providers to our website to register for our webinars. Webinars will be conducted by BDM (business development managers). Business development managers will then be given the task to work with our software development team to rapidly deploy service providers.

What is this Selling Thing of Which You Speak?

Obviously, all companies began as startups, which is sometimes easy to forget. In these nascent stages of the company's life as a startup, the focus needs to be on refining the business model with a laser focus on customer acquisition (sales growth). Without that focus on sales, startups either die or bounce along the road without ever truly thriving. During this phase, business development/salespeople need to give customers the white glove treatment. The white glove treatment leads to increased revenue and referrals, and the cycle continues.

However, as these startups grow into mature organizations, processes are tightened to increase efficiencies, employees develop specializations, products are refined, and services are delivered in fewer steps. Typically, disconnects begin to appear between customers and the company.

These disconnects also cause employees to be further and further removed from the customers—their needs, problems with products and services, ideas for product improvements, etc. As a result, in many organizations, large swaths of employees are completely out of touch with customers. They also either lose, or never had, a focus on sales.

"Sales" is in the job description of every single person in a startup. If you are an army of one, your primary goal is continuing to grow the business. It isn't adding one more feature to the UI (user interface). It isn't creating a pitch deck for investors that you will begin pitching in two months. **It is sales,**

plain and simple. If you have engineers, they need to focus on product development. Your software engineers need to be responsive to urgent needs to change the user experience. If you have finance people, they need to keep a very close eye on your cash flow. But if the entire team isn't committed to growing the company through sales, ultimately the startup will never take off.

I spoke with Kathy Hust, a former regional vice president for U.S. Cellular. Kathy led 2,800 sales and operations team members, and she consistently drove-double digit YOY (year-over-year) growth at U.S. Cellular. She also was the president of a rapidly growing early-stage company, Scanalytics. She also mentors startups on a regular basis. Kathy discussed with me her concern regarding the lack of focus on sales at many startups.

"Sometimes when I am mentoring startups, I am shocked at the lack of recognition of the importance of sales. At times, founders focus too much on product development; meanwhile, they are burning through cash and not growing the business. At one startup, the college student founders and I had regular meetings where we discussed the primary activities from the previous week.

At each meeting, I asked for an update on sales results. During one particular meeting one of the founders stated, "Well, we had a call last week from X company (a Fortune 500 company) that wanted to buy our product." I responded, "That is fantastic, where are we at with them? What are the next steps?" The response I received from one of the founders shocked me. "Well, we told them that we were too busy working with a supplier and didn't have the time to meet with them." Needless to say, we had a very direct conversation about how critical sales were to their business and that if they continued down this same path, they were simply not going to survive."

Startup Insight: Sales is the ultimate priority in a startup. Sales is in EVERYONE's job description in a startup.

---

3) Marketing Efforts: Inbound vs Outbound

When working to capture leads for the members of your sales team, deploy both inbound and outbound marketing tactics. The goal of these tactics is simple, attract people who are otherwise unfamiliar with your offering, nurture them until they set up a demo or make a purchase and finally, provide support after the purchase. In the case of Senior Aid, we need to drive traffic to our website to register for demos, so we'll focus on the tactics below.

Outbound:

1) Paid Search Campaigns

Internet paid search campaigns (e.g. Google AdWords) will assist in driving website traffic. This process involves using Google's Keyword Estimator Tool, ad creation and launch. Each campaign can be geo-targeted. This means campaigns will appear in designated areas based on IP address.

2) Trade Shows

Trade shows will become a critical component of future marketing efforts to medical service centers. We will need to identify the most efficient and effective conferences to drive the most sign-ups.

3) Social Media Ads

We will use the targeting options on social media to narrow our reach to seniors and their families. We will serve both images and video content related to in-home senior care and will direct viewers to our website. We will then use custom audiences and retargeting ads to reach those who have visited our site until they setup a demo.

4) Public Relations (PR)

Public relations efforts will target large market media outlets and the American Association of Retired Persons (AARP). We will also reach out to local media outlets with the success stories of the seniors we serve.

5) Email Marketing

We will use forms on our website to capture the email addresses of our visitors. We will set up automated email marketing campaigns to engage with our target audience on an ongoing basis.

We will start by providing resources such as "The ultimate guide to choosing the right level of in-home care for your loved one," or "The top 10 things needed for the most comfortable in-home care," and progressively ask for more involvement, such as an initial needs call and ultimately a demo.

Inbound:

1) Social Media Organic Content

YouTube: Our social media efforts will be driven by videos and testimonials from families. We will have separate software demo videos for home health care providers.

Facebook: We will utilize Facebook as our customer engagement platform. It will be critical not only to provide customer experience videos and tips for caring for loved ones, but also to monitor posts for potential customer problems.

We will also publish short-form content on Facebook that covers the life stories of the seniors we service and the caregivers who provide the servicing. This will help build an emotional connection with our audience and expand our reach.

2) Blog Posts

We will develop a series of blogs related to the most commonly asked questions about in-home senior care. To find these topics, we'll use a service like Answer The Public or Google Trends. Here is an example of the results:

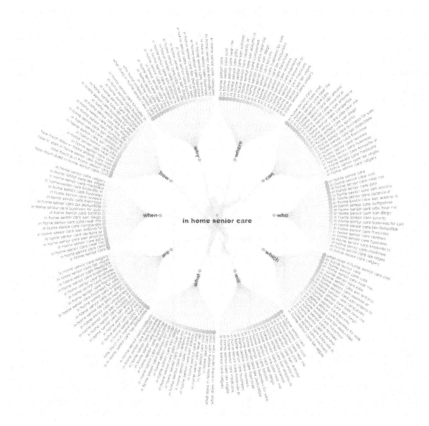

Important Note When setting up the marketing plan for your startup, determine what your competitors are doing. Pay special attention to the channels they are present on and the specific ways they are positioning their offering. Sign up for their email newsletter, their webinars and their demos. Do not simply copy the actions they are taking; learn from them.

In the past, I've found that most of the leads come from one or two sources. Try to figure out where the gaps are and focus on owning those channels. If they have the most engagement on YouTube and webinars, but don't have any paid search campaigns or content on Facebook, try developing content there first.

Lastly, you need to coordinate all of these activities. You most likely have a small team of people, or it might just be you, so creating a marketing calendar is critical. Managing your marketing without a plan will lead to missed sales opportunities and could even be fatal to your startup.

So, take the time to create a marketing calendar. Even something very basic like this:

Marketing Calendar (1st quarter)

	Jan	Feb	Mar	Person Responsible	Notes:
Tradeshow				Tom	Research most cost-effective trade shows.
Business Development			X	Mary & Bob	Hire Mary & Bob full-time by Mar 1.
Paid Search Advertising	X	X	X	Eli	Set up monthly budget by Dec 15.
Social Media		X	X	Sam and Anna	Provide 2 posts per week on Facebook and Twitter. Upload campaign videos to Facebook. Respond to new follows and messages.
Channel Partnerships			X	Kristen, Bob	Launch betas on recommended channels from AARP.
Associations			X	Dave	Join 1-2 associations to gather contacts and begin business development efforts.

STEP
06

Law School for Your Startup

Step 6 – Law School for Your Startup

I spoke with Hank Barry who is the head of Sidley Austin's Emerging Companies and Venture Capital practice group in Palo Alto. He was also a co-founder of the firm's Palo Alto office. He has advised many prominent technology companies as a lawyer, investor (partner at Hummer Winblad) and director. He was involved in seven of these companies from formation through IPO. He has testified twice before the U.S. Senate Judiciary Committee with respect to technology and intellectual property policy. Oh, and he was also the former CEO of Napster, so he has been through the startup grind.

The first topic Hank and I discussed was the issue of preparing new co-founders—those who have no startup experience—before they meet with their law firm for the first time.

"Most first-time entrepreneurs make similar missteps. When they launch their second and third companies, they have learned lessons from those mistakes.

One of the common issues I see with co-founders is they have not worked out their internal roles—who is expected to do what—employee, director, company officer. Often, they have not talked through who is going to receive what amount of equity. These are sometimes tough conversations, but essential. Sometimes these conversations result in someone leaving. That's okay, but it has to be reflected in writing to avoid problems later.

The second thing I find is that founders could be much more thoughtful about the form of entity they will use. Founders typically form a C corporation, and that works in most situations where institutional investment is the goal. But they should also think about the benefits of a pass-through entity like an LLC, at least in the early days of the company.

Getting this right can make a huge difference later. It's like a rocket ship; if you are three degrees off at the launch, you end up in the wrong ocean.

Lastly, some entrepreneurs spend too much time focusing on the easy issues—venture capital, IP issues, parsing of equity, future dilution etc.—all of the "internal" questions. This is understandable, but I find that focusing on these easy issues is an escape from facing the real issues—like the product is not working or we have no customers. If there are product problems and you don't fix them, you don't have to worry about equity dilution, because there won't be a company."

There are five primary areas of legal consideration for the startup.

1. Structure of the entity
2. Contracts
3. Compliance and licensing
4. Intellectual property (IP)
5. Funding

Legal Structure Options

Sole Proprietorship

A sole proprietorship is easy to form and gives you complete control of your business. You're automatically considered to be a sole proprietorship if you do business activities but don't register as any other kind of business. Sole proprietorships do not produce a separate business entity. This means your business assets and liabilities are not separate from your personal assets and liabilities. You can be held personally liable for the debts and obligations of the business. Sole proprietors are still able to get a company name, even though it isn't a legal entity. It can be hard to raise money since you can't sell stock, and banks are hesitant to lend to sole proprietorships. Sole proprietorships can be a good choice for low-risk businesses and owners who want to test their business idea before forming a more formal business.

Partnership

A partnership is the simplest structure for two or more people to own a business together. There are two common kinds of partnerships: limited partnerships (LP) and limited liability partnerships (LLP). Limited partnerships have only one general partner with unlimited liability, and all other partners have limited liability. The partners with limited liability also tend to have limited control over the company, which is documented in a partnership agreement. Profits are passed through to personal tax returns, and the general partner—the partner without limited liability—must also pay self-employment taxes. Limited liability partnerships are similar to limited partnerships, but give limited liability to every owner. An LLP protects each partner from debts against the partnership, and they won't be responsible for the actions of other partners. Partnerships can be a good choice for businesses with multiple owners, professional groups (like attorneys), and groups who want to test their business idea before forming a more formal business.

Limited Liability Company (LLC)

An LLC lets you take advantage of the benefits of both the corporation and partnership business structures. LLCs protect you from personal liability in most instances. This means your personal assets, like your vehicle, house and savings accounts, won't be at risk in case your LLC faces bankruptcy or lawsuits.

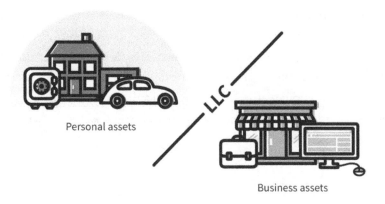

Personal assets

Business assets

Profits and losses can get passed through to your personal income without facing corporate taxes. However, members of an LLC are considered self-employed and must pay self-employment tax contributions toward Medicare and Social Security. LLCs can have a limited life in many states. When a member joins or leaves an LLC, some states may require the LLC to be dissolved and re-formed with new membership—unless there's already an agreement in place within the LLC for buying, selling and transferring ownership. LLCs can be a good choice for medium- or higher-risk businesses, owners with significant personal assets they want to be protected, and owners who want to pay a lower tax rate than they would pay with a corporation.

Corporations

C Corp

A C corporation is a legal entity that is separate from its owners. Corporations can make a profit, be taxed be held legally liable. A corporation offers the strongest protection to its owners from personal liability, but the cost to form a corporation is higher than other structures. Corporations also require more extensive record keeping, operational processes and reporting. Unlike sole proprietors, partnerships and LLCs, corporations pay income tax on their profits. In some cases, corporate profits are taxed twice—first, when the company makes a profit, and again when dividends are paid to shareholders on their personal tax returns.

Corporations have completely independent lives separate from their shareholders. If a shareholder leaves the company or sells his or her shares, the C corp can continue doing business relatively undisturbed. Corporations have an advantage when it comes to raising capital, because they can raise funds through the sale of stock, which can also be a benefit in attracting employees. Corporations can be a good choice for medium- or higher-risk businesses, businesses that need to raise money, and businesses that plan to "go public" or eventually be sold.

S Corp

An S corporation, sometimes called an S corp, is a special type of corporation that's designed to avoid the double taxation drawback of a regular C corp. An S corp allows profits, and some losses, to be passed through directly to the owner's personal income without ever being subject to corporate tax rates. Not all states tax S corps equally, but most recognize them the same way the federal government does, therefore taxing the shareholders accordingly. Some states tax S corps on profits above a specified limit, while others don't recognize the S corp election at all; they simply treat the business as a C corp.

S corps must file with the IRS to get S corp status, which is a different process than registering with their state. There are special limits on S corps. S corps can't have more than 100 shareholders, and all shareholders must be U.S. citizens. You will still have to follow strict filing and operational processes of a C corp. S corps also have an independent life, just like C corps. If a shareholder leaves the company or sells his or her shares, the S corp can continue doing business relatively undisturbed. S corps can be a good choice for businesses that would otherwise be a C corp, but meet the criteria to file as an S corp.

B Corp

A benefit corporation, sometimes called a B corp, is a for-profit corporation recognized in a majority of U.S. states. B corps are different from C corps in purpose, accountability and transparency, but aren't different in how they're taxed. B corps are driven by both mission and profit. Shareholders hold the company accountable to produce some sort of public benefit in addition to a financial profit. Some states require B corps to submit annual benefit reports that demonstrate their contributions to the public good. There are several third-party B corp certification services, but none are required for a company to be legally considered a B corp in those states where the legal status is available.

Close Corporation

Close corporations resemble B corps but have a less traditional corporate structure. These shed many formalities that typically govern corporations and those that apply to smaller companies. State rules vary, but shares are usually barred from public trading. Close corporations can be run by a small group of shareholders without a board of directors.

Nonprofit Corporation

Nonprofit corporations are organized to do charitable, educational, religious, literary or scientific work. Because their work benefits the public, nonprofits can receive tax-exempt status, meaning they don't pay state or federal income taxes on any profits they make.

Nonprofits must file with the IRS to get tax exemption, which again is a different process from registering with their state. Nonprofit corporations need to follow organizational rules very similar to a regular C corp. They also need to follow special rules about what they do with any profits they earn. For example, they can't distribute profits to members or political campaigns. Nonprofits are often called 501(c)(3) corporations—a reference to the section of the Internal Revenue Code that is most commonly used to grant tax-exempt status.

Source: Small Business Administration, 10/7/2017

Registering for an LLC example:

I cannot provide legal advice as to which legal entity type you should select. However, since I needed to set up a legal entity for a new company of mine, Startup Guides (Startupguides.io), I thought I would share the process I followed. Startup Guides provides startup training programs and mentoring, and it will serve as the publishing company for this and future books.

The ease and cost of filing for legal entity status does vary by state. Wisconsin happens to make this process very simple, affordable and fast. I literally completed the forms on the Wisconsin Department of Financial Institutions website in 10 minutes, paid $130, and my filing went off for approval. I received approval with the official designation of the legal entity status of Startup Guides LLC within five business days. Below is the initial screen of the process to file for Startup Guides LLC. You will notice at the beginning of this book that this material is copyrighted and owned by that business with the designation © 2017-Startup Guides LLC.

Note: Some states will charge closer to $1,000 and may take up to two months to process. So, if you are in need of creating immediate legal status for your company (like when you have an urgent contract), plan accordingly.

Contracts

Contracts can be very intimidating to the first-time entrepreneur. There are non-competes, non-disclosure agreements, operating agreements, license agreements, independent contractor agreements, project financing agreements and more.

There are four categories of contracts:

1. Commercial contracts
2. Human resources contracts
3. Transactional contracts
4. Intellectual property (IP) contracts

This table lists contract examples within each category:

Commercial	Human Resources	Transactional	Intellectual Property (IP)
• Vendor • Customer • Franchise • Marketing • Outsourcing • Supply • Procurement • Operations	• Founders • Employee • Consultancy • Non-compete • Non-solicitation • Stock option	• Joint Venture • Merger and Acquisition • Investments • Shareholder • Concession • Project Financing	• Non-disclosure • License • Assignment • Technology Transfer • Data Protection

I will explain some of the contracts that are generally most important during the startup phase. Note that sometimes the term "agreements" is used instead of "contracts." This is softer and less intimidating language and generally more widely used. Going forward in the book, we will be using the term agreements, not contracts.

Founders' Agreements - Written agreements that govern the relationship between the founders. These agreements are critical. It is extremely rare when founders decide to leave their company at the same time. People quit, get fired, get divorced, die, etc. Not planning for these scenarios is a bad idea. It is critical that founders put an agreement in place as soon as they begin their business relationship.

Customer Agreements - Written agreements between a buyer and a seller. First-time entrepreneurs frequently fall into the trap of doing business on a handshake when they are desperate for new business. This makes them appear unprofessional and unprepared and has many other negative ramifications (e.g. nonpayment).

Independent Contractor Agreements - Written agreements between a company and an independent contractor. Many startups also do business with a handshake when it comes to independent contractors. There are many bad reasons for not getting an agreement in place. One of the primary reasons is clarifying the point that they are employed as "work for hire" and that your startup owns the work that the independent contractors create (in return for payment). It is worth reiterating that you need to be extremely careful not to classify people as contractors when they should be classified as employees. Non-disclosure agreements and non-solicitation provisions should be included within independent contractor agreements.

Investor Agreements - Agreements between investors and current business owners that describe the terms of the investment, in addition to those for reporting and control.

Non-Disclosure Agreements (NDA) - Written agreements that protect the intellectual property of the owner. There are two types:

1. **Unilateral NDA** - Agreement whereby one party agrees not to reveal information to another party.
2. **Mutual NDA** - Agreement whereby both parties agree not to reveal information to another party.

Non-Compete Agreements - Agreement where an employee or other party (such as an independent contractor) agrees not to work for or start a similar company over a specified amount of time and within a geographical area.

I spoke with Chris Cain, partner with Foley and Lardner, LLP and co-founder of the nonprofit startup accelerator, Catapult Chicago, who was the attorney for one of my startups. Chris not only provides pragmatic insights for entrepreneurs, but is also a great strategist. He helps guide entrepreneurs through negotiations with suppliers, customers, investors and more.

I asked Chris about his insights into non-compete agreements and IP (Intellectual Property) for the startup.

"I discourage startup clients from asking for non-competes or signing non-competes. As a general rule, non-competes should only be considered in the context of selling the business, because at that point, the buyer is entitled to know the seller(s) will not be competing with the business post-sale for a period of time. In the employment context, many states will not enforce non-compete provisions, and those states that do enforce them only do so when very narrowly defined. Hence, it is better to avoid them. For employees of startup clients, I suggest that they instead use agreements that contain non-solicitation (e.g. no poach) provisions for employees and customers. These provisions are much more likely to be enforced by courts and get at what is of most concern when an employee leaves the company.

Regarding employees and intellectual property—as a startup, you will want to ensure your employees sign agreements that contain confidentiality provisions, and provisions indicating that all intellectual property they conceive in their scope of working for you, belongs to the company.

The concept of employers owning employees' intellectual property created in the scope of employment is widespread. While protective of you as a startup, it can also be potentially damaging to your business when hiring employees who have signed a similar agreement with their former employers. The risk is that the new employee brings to your startup some idea, technology, concept, etc. that their former employer may claim belongs to them. Hence, the agreement you have them sign as new employees should also contain a provision indicating they are not violating any other agreement and are not bringing with them any intellectual property they don't own. While this does not guarantee your startup won't face an action from a former employer of the new employee, it shows you made a good faith effort to prevent such an issue, and it may result in the former employer just pursuing the employee and not your company as well. As a practical matter, if a potential new employee's responsibilities for your startup will closely mirror what they did for their previous employer, consider if you want to take on the potential risk of them bringing confidential information and/or intellectual property of their former employer with them."

Note: The views expressed in this book by Mr. Cain are his personal opinions and views, and not those of Foley & Lardner, LLP or Catapult Chicago.

Intellectual Property

There are four categories of Intellectual Property (IP) that every entrepreneur needs to understand:

1. Trademarks
2. Copyrights
3. Patents
4. Industrial Designs

1) Trademarks - A word, brand name or symbol to indicate the owner. There are two types of trademarks: registered trademarks and unregistered trademarks. Trademarks for unregistered **products** utilize the ™ designation. The ™ stands for "trademark." Trademarks for unregistered **services** utilize the SM designation. The SM stands for "service mark."

Product Example: If you wanted to denote a trademark for a brand of sunglasses, a product, you would use ™ after your brand name.

Service Example: If you wanted to denote a trademark for software as a service (SaaS), you would utilize SM after your brand name.

Although federal registration of a mark is not mandatory, it has several advantages, including notice to the public of the registrant's claim of ownership of the mark, legal presumption of ownership nationwide, and exclusive right to use the mark on or in connection with the goods/services listed in the registration. You do need federal registration in order to file a lawsuit against someone you accuse of infringement.

Once trademarks are registered with the United States Patent and Trademark Office, both products and services use the ® designation. Registration is mandatory for protection.

As with all other legal areas with your business, consult your attorney.

2) Copyrights - Rights granted to the creator of literary, dramatic, musical, artistic or other intellectual works. Registration is not mandatory for protection.

Copyright of this book example: You will notice near the beginning of this book, it states the copyright ©2019 - Startup Guides LLC. This provides notification that the content of this book cannot be reproduced without the permission of my startup training and publishing company, Startup Guides LLC. As a side note, you have probably noticed already, I am here to help entrepreneurs, so I will most likely be very accommodating if you do decide to reproduce a portion of the book, as long as you get written permission from my company first.

3) Patents - Right granted for an invention that provides a new, unique product or process. In order to receive patent protection, registration is mandatory.

Patent example: The Apple Ring patent outlines plans to develop a smart, interactive ring that syncs with other Apple devices such as the iPhone or iPad, and can alert the wearer when a text, tweet or status update is received. In the place of a traditional jewel or stone, there is a touchpad touchscreen and the ring could also include a microphone for picking up voice commands.

4) Industrial Designs - New product or packaging design in the form of a shape, configuration, pattern or composition that is either two-dimensional (2D) or three-dimensional (3D). For protection, registration is mandatory.

Industrial design example: Coca Cola's contour bottle.

Tax Compliance

Your startup business (whether or not incorporated) is subject to federal, state and local tax compliance requirements from the time it is formed.

Relevant areas of tax compliance include:

a) federal and state corporate income tax
b) payroll taxes
c) real and personal property taxes
d) sales tax and the like

You need to be sure you have obtained applicable taxpayer identification numbers, such as a federal employer identification number (EIN), so you are properly registered at the state and local level. It's also important to understand what filings and other compliance are required. Startup-friendly tax accountants are typically the best places to provide this advice to startups, since they can address your ongoing tax return filing obligations as well as the initial registrations.

Investor Documentation

If you accept investments from friends and family or other third parties, you will need to document the terms of those investments and also get advice about securities law. Convertible debt or simple agreements for future equity (SAFEs) are frequently used at the very early stages to minimize legal expenses and avoid the need for more detailed investor arrangements. However, the terms of these agreements, which create rights designed to convert into convertible preferred stock in the future, are beyond the scope of this book. See your attorney.

Employment

In addition to payment and withholding of payroll taxes, you will be subject to other mandatory requirements in respect to employees, including procurement of workers' compensation and unemployment compensation insurance. Make sure you understand those obligations. Use of startup-friendly professional employer organizations (PEOs) can be a cost-effective way for early stage companies to deal with these requirements.

Insurance

Finally, you should get advice from an insurance broker as to the kinds of business insurance that are appropriate for a startup at your stage. The U.S. is a litigious country, and you need to consider what insurance you wish to procure even at a very early stage.

Source: Gust, Bob Mollen - Fried, Frank, Harris, Shriver & Jacobson

Licensing

The Basic Concept of Licensing:

To license is simply to grant another person the right to use some asset one owns for a particular purpose and, usually, for a particular payment or series of payments termed a "royalty." Most commonly, a party licenses the right to sell or exploit some business asset that one owns, such as intellectual property, a product or a methodology. A few examples include: a license to develop and promote a patented product and sell that same product in a particular territory; a license to use one's product as part of a blend of products that are sold; a license to utilize a trade name or logo to sell a product in a particular locale; the license to publish a copyrighted work one has written, etc.

The license is usually reduced to a written contract specifying the rights, duties, and payments that are part of the license. A license can give all rights to exploit the asset to the licensee ("exclusive licensee") or only some of the rights to use in conjunction with other persons ("nonexclusive" or "limited" license.) The license normally grants full rights to the licensee to exploit as the licensee sees fit, but may have certain performance criteria or a date when the license lapses or becomes nonexclusive.

Normally, the theme of a license is that the licensor is passive, merely receiving royalty payments, while the licensee engages in the business or development and is free to exploit so long as royalties are paid and other criteria are met. Failure to abide by the license agreement by the licensee normally results in termination of the license, as well as payment of damages to the licensor.

Unlike the sale of an asset, the licensor continues as the ultimate owner of the asset or methodology; limited rights to use what the licensor owns are transferred, but not ownership. The alternative to a license is the actual sale of the asset to the purchaser, but most licensors wish to continue as owners, so that they may exploit the asset in the future or in other territories or applications. It is vital for the licensee to realize that unlike full ownership, the license is merely a group of rights that the licensee obtains with ownership of the whole remaining with the licensor.

Typical Licensing Issues to Confront:

Who Owns What? It is vital to define precisely what rights are being licensed and for how long and in what context. If the licensor owns the other assets or concepts that the licensor is exploiting on its own or transferring to third parties, it is important to make full disclosure so that the licensee does not claim that it is facing competition from licensor's other activities and that the license is valueless. Related to this are variations and improvements on the product or concept, discussed below.

How Long, What Price? What does the licensor get from the license? What payments are due when? Is there any guaranteed amount or just a percentage of sales? How are sales computed? How long does it last? What performance criteria must the licensee accomplish to maintain the license? How can the licensee abandon the license and move on to other products and can either the licensor or licensee compete with the product or method with their own or a third party's product or method?

Who Defends What? Particularly with trade names or intellectual property, it is important to define who has the duty to defend against third parties violating rights to the intellectual property, and that can be an expensive process. For example, if the licensor licenses a software design that a third-party claims was stolen, who must defend the claim and pay any damages? This should all be defined precisely in the agreement.

Improvements and Changes. Assuming that the licensor develops an improvement or the next generation of product, does the licensee have the right to exploit that improvement? This is vital to consider since the licensee may create a thriving business, only to discover that the licensor has licensed a new product which utterly undercuts the business created by the licensee. Further, if the licensee comes up with a variation or improvement, does that generate any rights in the licensor?

Role of Other Licensees. If the license is nonexclusive, what protections may exist to stop the other licensee from interfering with sales of the current licensee? How are disputes between the licensees resolved?

Right to Assign? Right to Co-Venture? Often the licensee will wish to bring in other entities to assist in its efforts to promote the product or service or will seek to sell its own license to another party. What rights does the licensor have to object or approve of such steps?

Right of Licensee to Alter the Product or Service. Typically, a licensee comes up with its own ideas or variations to the licensed product, either alone or in conjunction with third parties or when a customer requests a customized variation. What rights does the licensee have to alter the product or service?

Advertising and Promotional Materials. Often a licensor will want approval rights as to all marketing, training and advertising materials. Usually, the licensee wants freedom of action and does not want the licensor, who may not be well versed in marketing or local conditions, to have veto power.

Indemnity Provisions. Most licensors want full protection, including insurance coverage, for the activities of the licensees. Most licensees want product liability carried by the licensor. The extent of such provisions is often an area of tense negotiations.

Local Regulations and Laws. Many locales, especially Europe, have extremely strict regulations as to products and services and restrictions on the right to trade and sell. Indeed, often local law can void contrary provisions in the license agreement. Some products considered safe and legal in a particular jurisdiction are illegal in others. A good example is alcohol sold in some Arab nations. It is vital to check applicable laws and regulations.

Taxes and Licenses. It is equally vital to allocate who is responsible for what taxes that may accrue. Normally, the licensee wants to not be involved in sales or employment activities and wants to be held harmless from all such liabilities. To achieve that, careful attention must be paid to the structure created in the agreement, since some jurisdictions may impose pseudo employment taxation in certain license arrangements. Of course, local business licenses must be paid and kept up to date by the licensee.

Standard Contract Issues. In addition to the numerous applicable issues that a particular project must consider, the standard terms and conditions and issues relating to them in any business contract must be considered.

Why License?

There are numerous other methods to join efforts to promote and sell a product or service, ranging from joint ownership of a single entity to joint ventures (partnerships of two or more entities) to distribution and sales representative arrangements. In most cases, a license is the method preferred by a person or entity who simply wants an entirely passive role. An example is receiving royalties, with no involvement in the day-to-day or even strategic marketing decisions. As one client put it, "I just want to sit back and cash my royalty checks."

But it is seldom that simple. The activities of the licensee must be of keen interest to any wise licensor, since a bad or poorly performing licensee can result in a product or service that could have developed a good cash flow becoming useless, while other competing products come to dominate the field. Further, most licensees need guidance and assistance from the licensor, so inevitably more than "cashing the checks" is involved. While many inventors dream of licensing their product to some multinational that will simply pay a great deal of money over time, the average license involves two relatively small businesses who have to work together to make the process successful.

Licensing a product or service can be an excellent way to generate good cash flow if the document is properly created. This means there is a clear understanding of the goals and duties of both parties. More often than not, a license is limited in scope so that the licensor is free to develop certain markets or work with more than one licensee. It is vital to keep not only good legal advice in mind, but to get good tax advice and local knowledge before commencing the relationship. If done well, an inventor or developer of a product or service can minimize his or her involvement in the work of marketing and delivering the service or product, while still receiving a good income.

Source: Stimmel, Stimmel & Smith P.C.

STEP
07

Raising Capital for Your Startup

Step 7 – Raising Capital for Your Startup

My $200 Seed Round

I worked at Humana as a marketing manager on the personal health insurance side of the business. The decision was made, wisely, to combine the marketing departments of the personal health insurance and the small group insurance sides. The new office was located two hours away and my wife, Amy, and I were not about to move our family. Little did I know that the entrepreneurial vehicle inside me was revving its engine.

My salary at Humana made-up roughly 60 percent of our household income. I began searching for other corporate jobs, and while looking, bile literally starting coming up in the back of my mouth. I could not go back to corporate. I felt it in my gut; I needed to chart my own path with my own startup. Amy and I discussed my dream of having my own business. She supported the decision to launch Sales Sherpas. I was so confident in the business model, based on my previous experience and somewhat naive bravado, that I said I only needed $200 in seed money. That would cover the cost of a logo and 500 business cards. There were many twists and turns, mistakes and successes, but eventually that $200 investment swelled to $750k in revenue. For my first company with a battalion of one and extremely low overhead, I was quite proud. It wasn't until later that I realized the successes from Sales Sherpas contributed to my subsequent seed round of $500k in my next startup just four years later.

But there were financial challenges along the way to which I was completely naive. Startups put financial pressure on families, and that was something I had not considered when I launched the company. I applied this lesson to my subsequent companies. Next, I should have considered the amount of cash we had available to invest. Then, I should have considered the minimum amount of monthly cash that would be required to support my family. (It's important to note that I am not focusing on revenue or profit.) Then, in the event that the business was not self-sustaining, I should have considered other sources of cash I could rapidly raise.

My First Cash Flow Crunch

I distinctly remember being in a cash crunch due to a large customer paying late and the need to pay a software developer and graphic designer. This meant I was not going to be able to bring home a paycheck for our family (remember, entrepreneurs get paid last). Amy and I could have tapped a home equity line of credit, our 401(k)s or friends and family. We agreed that we would not go down those paths. So, I went to branches of two national banks, one local bank and one regional bank in our city, to seek a $10k line of credit. At the time, I had generated about $170k in revenue with about $80k in net profit (my salary). I was turned down flatly at all locations. Even after bringing a comprehensive business plan and doing business at the national bank for over 10 years (with a spotless record), they refused. The regional bank offered me a corporate credit card with a $4k limit and I took it. I harbored resentment against these banks for a long period of time. Eventually, I became more philosophical about the situation and realized how risk averse they had become after the economic meltdown of 2008. I am not going to go down the path of the blame game for 2008. There were many bad decisions made by many countries, many companies and many individuals. We move forward and hopefully learn our lessons.

Amy and I did agree to not use credit cards, but frankly, sometimes there are no other options to fund a business. So we moved on and shortly thereafter paid off the credit card.

Critical Financial Discussions

I learned a few lessons from my first cash flow crunch and the lack of my preparedness. Specifically, I learned lessons that will help you as you plan.

Here are some initial financial questions to help you plan for the life of your startup:

1. How much money are you and your spouse/significant other willing to invest in the startup?
2. Do you have a monthly family budget? If not, it is very important to create one, now. What costs are you willing to cut from your family budget?
   a. Fewer family vacations?
   b. Decreased contributions to your children's college fund?
   c. Not purchasing a new car?
3. How long are you willing to go without a paycheck?
4. What are your sources of income to cover the budget of the business, if any?
5. Does your spouse/significant other need to get a job or a higher-paying job to make this happen?
6. What are the financial triggers that will cause you to shut down the business? $10k in debt? Not generating a paycheck for 6 months? Exhausting your $30k home equity line of credit?

Startup Insight: Have the conversations about family finances well before you launch your startup. It will make life a great deal less stressful and minimize the risk of putting your family in dire financial straits.

There are many methods to raise capital so you can fund your startup. These options are not mutually exclusive of one another. Also, note that as you move from a startup idea to a living, breathing startup and then on to an early-stage company, your choice of funding options will expand.

There are a few primary options to raise capital for your startup:

1. Bootstrapping
2. Friends, Fools and Family (3Fs)
3. Banks and credit unions
4. Community development financial institutions
5. Crowdfunding
6. Online lenders
7. Angel investors
8. Venture capitalists
9. SBIR grants
10. Pitch competitions

Bootstrapping

Bootstrapping, as the name implies, is the act of self-funding a startup. Some consider only funds from the entrepreneur as true bootstrap funds. Others will include 3Fs (Friends, Fools and Family) and others include crowdfunding.

Although bootstrapping can cause a startup to launch and grow at a slower pace than seeking outside funding, it can also create an over reliance on the startup capital and lead to the enabling of poor entrepreneurial decision-making. Think of that rich kid whose parents showered him/her with cash, never allowing their child to develop skills to become self-sufficient.

Bootstrapping forces entrepreneurs to move rapidly to revenue generation. They also must carefully manage cash for operations and hire only high-impact team members. These all increase the probability of long-term success for the startup.

Many first-time entrepreneurs don't have hundreds of thousands of dollars sitting in the bank to invest in their startups. Even if you do, your spouse/significant other might not have the appetite for taking a large bite out of your financial nest egg.

Some of the most common sources of personal funding include:

- Savings
- Home equity lines of credit
- Early retirement disbursements
- Credit cards

Taking early retirement disbursements is generally a last resort due to early withdrawal penalties and the loss of the compounding effect of your gains. Likewise, I don't advocate using high interest credit cards. However, the reality is that low-interest credit cards are frequently used. In general, post 2008, banks are extremely risk-averse and tend not to provide loans to startup companies. The old adage of, "banks only loan money to people who have it" frequently rings true.

Having a conversation with your spouse/significant other about the maximum investment you are both willing to make and the sources of the funds is crucial. I know of an entrepreneur who took on $20,000 in credit card debt without talking with his spouse, and it wreaked havoc on their marriage.

I recommend having easy access to a minimum of twelve months of cash to cover your family's living expenses. However, this is not always realistic.

Friend, Fools and Family Money (3Fs)

The second most popular source of startup funding behind self-funding is that of friends and family.

According to statistics on the Fundable crowdfunding website, friends and family are a major funding source for all entrepreneurs, investing over $60 billion in new ventures in 2016, almost triple the amount coming from venture capital sources. The average amount raised from venture capital sources per startup was $23k, usually in the form of a convertible loan, rather than an equity investment.

The benefits of using 3Fs funding include: rapid access to funds; money is frequently provided with no expectation of return of the capital, nor any interest; and they most commonly do not require the entrepreneur to provide equity in return for the capital.

Be aware that sometimes family members providing funds feel they have a strong influence on how the business should be run, even though they lack the startup experience and knowledge to guide the business.

One of the most significant challenges that entrepreneurs don't consider is the negative impact on relationships that occurs in the event that the startup folds. This is especially true when the entrepreneur does not have the funds to pay back family or friends.

When I am coaching entrepreneurs and the discussion of Friends and Family arises, I ask them the question, "Can you handle looking across the table at Thanksgiving and telling them that they won't be getting their money back?"

Banks & Credit Unions

Banks and credit unions are sometimes extremely conservative with the risk they are willing to take with small businesses, especially immediately post 2008. However, small/local banks and credit unions that are committed to local communities and interested in developing the local economy are generally going to be much more likely to loan you money than large, national banks.

"The number of small-business loans fell dramatically during the recession, as big banks cut off credit to customers they considered risky, and many smaller and regional banks that once lent to local business owners shut their doors. It's better now; in 2016, eight years after the crash, 45 percent of small-business owners reported receiving credit, up from 22 percent in 2014, according to the Federal Reserve."

Source: Inc. Magazine, Follow the Money, June 2017, Anna Hensel

Some of the key benefits of using banks and credit unions are that they can often provide lower interest rates than other lenders, they don't require any equity, and they tend to have higher customer satisfaction than that of online lenders.

Source: Federal Reserve 2017

Some banks and credit unions have high rejection rates. For example, in 2016, only 28 percent of businesses with less than $100k in annual revenue received the funds they sought.

Source: Small Business Credit Survey, Collaboration of 2 Federal Reserve Banks

Banks and credit unions can sometimes have laborious and very manual processes, and there is a general aversion to lending to startup companies (which are deemed as high risk). There are exceptions; business banks have become more prone to taking risks. Also, local banks run by forward-thinking bank executives with a strong stake in community growth tend to be more tolerant of startup loans.

Community Development Financial Institutions (CDFIs)

CDFIs are private financial institutions dedicated to providing loans to help residents start businesses, assist families with financing their first homes and investing in local health centers, schools or community centers.

Source: CDFIfund.gov

CDFIs are comprised of community development banks, community development loan funds and community development venture funds. CDFIs raise capital from individuals and institutions (banks, non-financial institutions (i.e. insurance companies), government, religious institutions, and foundations). There were between 8,000 and 10,000 CDFIs in the U.S. in 2016.

Source: Taking Stock, CDFIs Look Ahead After 25 Years of Community Development Finance.

Lenders to CDFIs (e.g. banks) were struck by the mortgage crisis of 2008, causing both the amount of funds channeled into CDFIs and the acceptance rate of applications to decline.

CDFIs have a direct interest in spurring their local economy; they tend to be less averse to risk than individual banks. They also provide a local network of other resources and tend to offer lower interest rates than the traditional market. CDFI application processes can sometimes be lengthy, and depending on the locale and relative economic conditions, funds can be limited.

Crowdfunding

Crowdfunding is the process of raising capital to fund a startup, product, invention, project, literary work, event or special cause through a web-based campaign on a specific crowdfunding platform. There are four types of crowdfunding platforms: Reward, Equity, Donation and Debt/Loan. If you decide to venture down the crowdfunding path, you need to match your startup type with the crowdfunding platform you choose. You should also consider particular nuances of each platform.

Types of Crowdfunding Services:

Reward Crowdfunding - A service whereby supporters of the campaign receive a tangible reward. Example: A donor to a Kickstarter campaign for a new solar powered smartphone might receive a free solar panel for their smartphone.

Equity Crowdfunding - A service whereby supporters (investors) receive equity in the firm they support. Example: An individual invests $10k in a startup on AngelList and they receive a 5 percent equity stake in the company. There are currently considerable limitations by states on who can "qualify" to invest in startups through equity crowdfunding.

Donation Crowdfunding - A service whereby supporters receive the psychological benefit of helping a specific cause or individual. Example: An individual creates a campaign on GoFundMe to raise money for hurricane victims.

Debt Crowdfunding - A service whereby supporters provide loans in return for the loan payment plus interest. Example: Individuals each provide support of $10k on Kiva for a woman launching a pottery business in Africa. Within 24 months, they expect to receive a return of the 10K, plus 8 percent interest.

We will focus on further explaining "reward crowdfunding" here. This type of crowdfunding provides the dual benefit of raising capital and simultaneously creating brand awareness with your crowdfunding campaign. Some platforms provide you the opportunity to make actual sales of your product (such as Kickstarter). This can be a tremendous way to conduct product validation.

Sometimes supporters of reward campaigns perceive themselves to be investors and try to make demands beyond that of receiving the product/service that they ordered. This can lead to tremendous distractions when the entrepreneur needs to be focused on growing the business. Creating an effective crowdfunding campaign can take a considerable amount of time. Spending time creating the copy (text) for the campaign is just the beginning.

The most effective campaigns have powerful, compelling videos to engage the campaign supporter. These can take time and money. Incidentally, I am a homebrewer and bought the "uKeg" pressurized [beer] growler after watching an entertaining and engaging video by Growlerwerks on Kickstarter. They did not spend a tremendous amount on the campaign, but created a compelling story that developed a tremendous amount of buzz (no pun intended) and yielded over 10,000 backers!

The uKeg Pressurized Growler for Fresh Beer

The uKeg™ growler keeps beer fresh and cold on the go. Vacuum insulated stainless steel with carbonation cap, pressure gauge and tap.

Shop Now

Created by
GrowlerWerks

10,293 backers pledged $1,559,525 to help bring this project to life.

Some crowdfunding services, such as Kickstarter, do not pay out the funds unless you hit your goal. So, setting an achievable goal is very important. Other crowdfunding platforms, such as Indiegogo, provide you the funds even if you don't achieve your goal. However, you need to consider the audience before selecting a crowdfunding service. Look at the products and services that are typically promoted on that particular crowdfunding service. More importantly, look at the campaigns that are exceeding their goals and clearly engaging supporters (you can see both a real-time view of the amount of money raised in the campaign and the number of supporters, aka backers).

The fee to use these crowdfunding services typically hovers around 5 percent, but it varies. This fee can be an important consideration if you are seeking to raise a great deal of money, and should be added to the amount you need to receive from the campaign itself.

Startup Insight: Not all crowdfunding services provide you your funds unless you hit your goal. Be sure to set a realistic target.

I spoke with Rob Kowalik, Practice Director, Healthcare Solutions at Blue Vision, which is a provider of wireless sensors and beacons with cloud connectivity.

Rob was a co-founder of a startup that created a portable video camera with cloud connectivity. Rob's startup raised an impressive $250k on Kickstarter.

"We started our business with friends and family money. I feel our Kickstarter campaign was a solid success. But most people launching a crowdfunding campaign do not understand all the work, time and money involved with a successful campaign. It is easy to take your focus off the business.

We must have been spending 50 percent of our time on the Kickstarter campaign up to two months before the campaign. Here are what people need to understand—60 percent of Kickstarter campaigns never get funded and the average one that does get funded raises $5,000. In order to really knock it out of the park, you need to commit significant capital up front. We spent 25 grand with a small ad agency in LA. They created a compelling video with a model of the camera and, more importantly, had us, the co-founding team, talking about the company and how the product would help our customers. We had bloggers pushing the campaign, press releases, social media posts, email blasts, webinars, and interviews with reporters.

You also have to have those initial customers already committed to support your campaign BEFORE you launch the campaign. Those that hit their targets typically achieve 40 percent of their campaign goal in the first 24 hours. We achieved 30 percent of ours in just 3 hours.

The other thing people don't understand is that campaign supporters think they own a share of the company, not just the product they ordered. They wanted insights into the company itself, financials, etc. We got bombarded with phone calls; they found our personal email addresses, and contacted us on social media. When we didn't deliver the product on time, we even received a call where the guy gave me a death threat!

Don't get me wrong, I think crowdfunding can be a very effective tool to help conduct market validation. We learned a great deal about what people wanted through not only the high level of support, but through conversations, through chat, etc. It's just that you have to go in realizing that you are probably going to have to take your eye off your business for a couple of months prior to the campaign, and then through the duration of the campaign, and then you also need to be prepared for the perceived control that a campaign supporter has over your company."

Online Lending

Not to be confused with crowdfunding, online lending provides loans directly to consumers and businesses. Lenders such as Lending Club, Kabbage, Funding Circle and OnDeck offer quick and easy loans. These online lenders are, in general, very enthusiastic about funding startups and small businesses (in addition to providing loans to individuals).

Online lending firms tend to have an easy application process and higher acceptance rates vs. traditional funding sources (e.g. banks and credit unions). However, they tend to provide relatively small amounts of capital and tend to charge very high interest rates.

Angel Investors

Angel investors tend to be high net-worth individuals or consortiums of high net-worth individuals. Geography can determine the amount an angel investor may be willing to provide. For example, in the U.S. Midwest, a general rule of thumb is that angel investors invest under $1 million. On the West or East Coasts, that number can move up to as much as $3 million. Once you get higher than those amounts, you typically move into venture capital or private equity investments.

There are two distinct types of angel investors relative to their ability to provide strategic guidance.

Dumb money - Individuals or small groups of individuals who possess capital to invest but do not possess domain expertise in your particular target market, product or service. The advantage of "dumb money" is that this type of money is much easier to find than "smart money."

Note: If you are trying to ensure you can't raise money from these people, refer to them as dumb money. The following statement would be a bad idea: *"You know we are really looking for smart money, but we can't find any, so we will take dumb money. When can we pick up the check?"*

Smart money - Individuals or, more commonly, consortiums of high net-worth individuals that focus on a specific sector. They possess domain expertise and only invest in that sector/domain.

Insights from Hyde Park Angels

Hyde Park Angels is one of the 10 largest angel groups in the U.S. and definitely would qualify as smart money. Hyde Park Angels is a consortium of a large group (in their case, over 130 investors as of Sept. 2017), who possess such a significant breadth of knowledge, they cover most sectors, based simply on probability.

Peter Wilkins, the managing director of Hyde Park Angels, discussed with me, what angel investors find attractive in startup investments.

"New entrepreneurs tend to think that the product or service needs to be perfect. They just want to keep adding whistles and bells. They come with over-engineered products. They don't understand the concept of an MVP (minimum viable product). They just want to keep adding feature after feature until they think it is perfect, without getting customer feedback.

We ask questions to validate the product or service idea. Such as: Tell me about the idea. What evidence do you have that people will change their behavior with your idea? If it is just a concept, tell me what industry experts have told you about the idea. If it is at MVP stage, tell me 10 key customers you have and give me evidence they are using it.

When you pitch to angels, get to the value proposition quickly; explain how you are going to help your customers. Show the angels the size of the market and how you think you can capture the market.

We had someone pitch us who spent over $400,000 of their own money or more to build a prototype, but hadn't even validated a need for the product. Then they came in with a crazy valuation just because they had put in hundreds of thousands of dollars.

One of the things that makes startups attractive is removing some of the risk in the investment. Serial successes obviously reduce that risk. This makes the potential investment much more palatable to the investor.

Final thought here ... I strongly believe businesses do not need to be "venture backed" to be considered a success. I have seen many individuals launch businesses with venture money ... and have built the businesses into solid $7 million - $8 million a year firms and have been perfectly happy. Then sometimes they sell those businesses and move onto something else."

Venture Capitalists

Venture capital is an investment made by a group of accredited investors in exchange for equity. These investors either contribute through a fund, or through a firm. Venture capitalists tend to invest in early-stage companies (post-startup phase). Angel investors typically invest in startups. As a result, venture capitalists tend to invest more capital than angel investors.

Investors in venture capital funds are typically very large institutions, such as pension funds, financial firms, insurance companies and university endowments—all of which put a small percentage of their total funds into high-risk investments. They expect a return of between 25-35 percent per year over the lifetime of the investment. Because these investments represent such a tiny part of the institutional investors' portfolios, venture capitalists have a lot of latitude. What leads these institutions to invest in a fund is not the specific investments, but the firm's overall track record, the fund's "story," and their confidence in the partners themselves.

Where venture money plays an important role is in the next stage of the innovation life cycle—the period in a company's life when it begins to commercialize its innovation. It is estimated that more than 80 percent of the money invested by venture capitalists goes into building the infrastructure required to grow the business—in expense investments (manufacturing, marketing, and sales) and the balance sheet (providing fixed assets and working capital).

Venture money is not long-term money. The idea is to invest in a company's balance sheet and infrastructure until it reaches a sufficient size and credibility so that it can be sold to a corporation, or so that the institutional public-equity markets can step in and provide liquidity. In essence, the venture capitalist buys a stake in an entrepreneur's idea, nurtures it for a short period of time, and then exits with the help of an investment banker.

Source: How Venture Capital Works, Bob Zider, Harvard Business Review

Grants

The Technology Program Office, which is part of the Small Business Administration (SBA), administers the Small Business Innovation Research (SBIR) Program and the Small Business Technology Transfer (STTR) Program. Through these two competitive programs, SBA ensures that the nation's small, high-tech, innovative businesses are a significant part of the federal government's research and development efforts. Eleven federal departments participate in the SBIR program; five departments participate in the STTR program, awarding collectively $2 billion to small high-tech businesses each year.

Source: SBA.gov, 10/17/17

Pitch Competitions

Pitch competitions are typically run by a university, another institution or a group seeking to foster growth in a specific geographic location or in a particular business sector.

The benefits of pitch competitions include: no distribution of equity, no loan repayment, provision of free public relations for your startup and exposure to future stakeholders (investors, mentors, customers, team members).

However, pitch competitions can be time consuming, which can take away from startup operations and other efforts to raise capital. In some competitions, there can be a low probability of winning (depending on the number and caliber of the competing startups).

If a pitch competition provides significant benefits (e.g. networking and access to the aforementioned stakeholders) beyond the competition winnings, then they can be an effective use of time. Be careful not to fall into the trap of applying for and participating in pitch competitions for the sake of your ego, at the risk of taking your eye off the ball (losing focus on the day-to-day operations). I know a startup founder who applied for every pitch competition possible, to the point where he wasn't paying attention to core issues of the startup that needed to be addressed. He was essentially rearranging the deck chairs on the Titanic.

STEP

08

Pitching Your Startup

Step 8 – Pitching Your Startup

What We Learned as Babies

ABC's *Shark Tank* and *Dragon's Den*, internationally, have spurred a global, unparalleled level of excitement about the field of entrepreneurship. It has become must-watch TV in many households around the world, including mine.

Beyond the products or services, themselves, we get to peer into the lives of many individuals who have faced personal hardships, tragedies and sacrifices and those who have committed themselves to taking control of their own destinies by creating solutions to problems or innovations.

I personally find the stories to be more compelling than the products or services themselves. People love to hear human stories, especially stories of people overcoming adversity. The stories could be about illnesses within a family or recovering from bankruptcy. Many startup stories begin with nothing, and then the protagonist (in this case, the entrepreneur) triumphs over their situation and we, along with the angel investors, want to help them move forward. These angel investor "sharks" or "dragons" choose to invest or not and we, in some cases, become their consumers by purchasing their products or services because we want to help those entrepreneurs.

When you create your startup idea, there is usually an immediate unbridled enthusiasm to share the idea with others. These people could be friends, family members, co-workers, potential employees, prospective investors and prospective customers, among others. Our emotional response is to blurt out a description in a sentence beginning with something like, "I had this amazing idea," "You have to check this out," "I can't wait to share this with you," "There is nothing else like this out there," etc. Instantly, a virtual barrier goes up and people tune us out, because they have heard these sentences so many times that they have become desensitized.

We are conditioned very early on in life to enjoy hearing stories from our parents. These stories entertained, engaged and provided comfort. Even the most battle-hardened angel investor or VC likes to hear a story. So, when we start discussing our startup ideas, instead of launching into one of those statements that cause people to tune out, we should begin with a story to help engage them. The stories need to be compelling, interesting and powerful in order to really grab the listener's attention. Begin by prefacing the narrative, saying you are going to tell them a story. A compelling story can engage your audience (for example, angel investors) right away.

The story obviously needs to be genuine, interesting, unique or powerful, and it needs to compel the person to act or react in some way. You might be trying to get feedback on your startup idea, make that initial sale, get someone to join your startup team or get an investment in your startup. A good story can improve the likelihood of these happening.

Creating your Pitch Deck

Once we have told our story, we need to move into a few time-tested steps that help the recipient efficiently and effectively understand our startup idea. Believe it or not, you should be able to compress this to under 90 seconds; this becomes your pitch. From this statement comes your value proposition.

Sometimes, you will hear the phrase, "an elevator pitch." This term is derived from the fact that a typical elevator ride is 30 seconds. You will find that most pitch competitions now are 90 seconds, which really forces the entrepreneur to be focused on their story and the startup idea itself. You will want to get your pitch down to 90 seconds too, regardless of who you are talking to about your startup idea. It doesn't matter whether it's a prospective investor, employee, customer, supplier or anyone else who could provide you insights to help grow your startup.

Here are the minimum core details you need in your pitch deck:

1. Your story
2. The market

3. Customer segment(s)
4. Size of the market and opportunity
5. The problem or unmet need
6. The solution
7. What your product or service is
8. How it works
9. Your team
10. Your milestones, including progress to date

If you are involved in formal pitches to investors, you will need to provide additional details including: The competition, your competitive advantage(s), your "Go to Market Strategy" (your sales and marketing efforts), and critical action items that need to be taken in the next 12 months. Lastly, you will need to share the amount of investment you are seeking (do not share the amount of equity you will provide—that will be dependent on the terms of the deal) and projections of growth.

We have included a very **well-crafted pitch deck as an example in the appendix for you**. The pitch deck is from Scanalytics, a floor sensor analytics company that transforms physical locations into smart environments. Scanalytics raised millions of dollars in venture capital with this deck.

Be very careful when creating your growth projections. Seasoned investors have seen thousands of pitch slides showing the proverbial "hockey stick" sales forecasts and have also seen most startups fail.

You need to have a science behind these forecasts. Have you already sold a certain number of units? Do you have purchase orders or letters of intent from customers? Even better, do you have revenue and measured customer growth? Do you have a sales "close rate" (percent of sales made relative to webinars, meetings, etc.) that you can use as a baseline? Some investors will even say they prefer not to see sales forecasts. Ask before you go into a pitch whether or not they would like to see sales projections.

Below are the Most Common Questions that Judges and Investors will ask you.

Instructions: Write down your answers and have these answers memorized. Pitching can be nerve wracking and quickly lead to pitches falling apart during the Question and Answer session.

1. How big is the market opportunity? Prove it with data and/or discovery you collected.
2. Can you justify that a problem – worth solving, with real data/interviews conducted – actually exists? Prove it.
3. Why are you and your team (if you have one) the people to solve the problem? Who are they, what is their experience that is relevant to your startup? Are there gaps in what the startup needs?
4. Will this solution really work? What is the proof, from research, that it could be adopted by real, paying customers? Note: The best-case scenario to justify your answer is that you have actual paying customers.
5. Do you have a **sustainable** competitive advantage? Be very careful if you think it is "low price" because, as your costs increase, generally your prices will need to increase as well.
6. Are your sales forecasts realistic? Prove it. Revenue is the ultimate proof.
7. Are your costs realistic? Prove it. With a startup, real revenue and real costs are the ultimate proof. Consider the overhead costs once you start growing, not just the costs of launching in your dorm or apartment.
8. How much is the realistic amount of money you need to conduct a pilot/beta? If you are an existing entity, how much do you need to accelerate the growth? Provide detail on how the money will be used (avoid large founder salaries). They want to see the money being directed toward growing the startup.
9. Have you considered what could go wrong? How would you address those issues?

10. Will we (the investors) get a return on our investment? Explain how and when you think that will happen (e.g., the sale of the company, royalties, etc.).

STEP
09

Building Your Startup Team

Step 9 – Building Your Startup Team

Growing From a Team of One

If you are deciding to create a "lifestyle" business where your primary goal is to maintain a specific standard of living, you can keep your organization very small—perhaps only a team of one. Examples of lifestyle businesses would include: small consulting, accounting or marketing firms. Keep in mind that without a marketing department, sales team, accounting department, operations, engineering, and administrative teams, and a vendor network, these tasks and operations are all your responsibility as well. Even lifestyle businesses typically expand to need employees.

One thing I've learned from my own startups is the ability to assess my own strengths and weaknesses. I went from participating in traditional leadership surveys, where only my employees evaluated me, to 360-degree feedback assessments. During my career as a manager working for Fortune 500 firms, I was accustomed to solid leadership reviews.

When I was in sales, I was a solid performer (received 12 Pacesetter Awards at BellSouth, sold the first wireless PBX, developed a sales territory from five clients to over 1,500 clients, etc.). In marketing, where I managed $6 million to $20 million-per-year marketing budgets, I almost always achieved our targets, managed marketing through thousands of sales agents, and nearly always came in under budget. I had learned some very valuable sales, marketing and management insights which "I knew" would hold me in good stead. I had a good idea of my strengths.

However, these successes didn't help me identify weaknesses and gaps in knowledge that quickly become painfully apparent in a startup. Although I had received accolades for leadership and awards for sales performance, I was never responsible for cash flow management; I didn't have to engage in complex projects; I wasn't involved in overseeing software development; I didn't have to work with investors; I didn't lead a board of directors.

Successful entrepreneurs possess the ability to learn from mistakes, acquire critical new knowledge and combine those to develop new skills that lead their startups to success.

I had a conversation with Peter Layton, who is one of the founding partners of <u>Blackthorne Capital Management</u>. Peter serves as chairman of the BOX Exchange Group, a partner of Efficient Capital Management, and a member of Hyde Park Angels. He was a partner at both The Hull Group and Goldman Sachs & Co.

I asked Peter for his insights into the characteristics and behaviors of founders that build highly scalable startups.

"There are essentially 10 behaviors I see in founders who scale their startups:

1. They have a clear vision. They are focused on a specific business model.
2. They have proven the market.
3. They are willing to pivot based on customer feedback.
4. They understand the cost of customer acquisition.
5. They minimize churn.
6. They generate revenue quickly and, therefore, market feedback.
7. They understand their own limitations and get help for areas of weakness.
8. They establish a good board early.
9. They make a capital-raising plan and stick to it by meeting milestones of firm performance.
10. They have the ability to communicate likely exits—investors want to know there is a way out."

Our conversation transitioned into the most common mistakes he sees founders making when selecting members of the core initial team. Peter continued:

"I find that some of the most common mistakes in hiring the initial team members are:

1. Not understanding their company's needs (and their weaknesses).
2. Underestimating the importance of marketing and the people required to market.
3. Giving away too much equity to people early, before understanding if those people are key success drivers.
4. Adopting nonstandard voting rights to protect early owners—one class of stock ... no complications.
5. Keeping friends on the team, even when they are no longer adding value.
6. Not judging people critically based on their knowledge, education, experience, network and integrity."

Management Lesson From Cancun

I launched my first startup, Sales Sherpas, as a team of one. I landed a $20,000 sale that was designated as a "marketing research" project, which turned out to be making thousands of cold calls for a telecom company, but the money was good. I put my sales skills to good use and I was off and flying. However, while I was focused on actually doing the work itself, I had not dedicated enough time to filling "the pipeline" with new prospects. In the past, I'd had other people creating and delivering the products and services I marketed and sold. Now, I was wearing a sales hat and an operations hat. The inevitable occurred; I finished up with the $20,000 project, and although I had "deals in the pipeline," none of them had closed. I landed some small marketing projects, a couple of $5,000 deals and $10,000 deals and really started to get back into "sales mode." Financially, I hadn't yet reached the level of income I had provided for my family when I was in corporate, but I was doing well enough to go on a family vacation to Cancun.

Being from Wisconsin, my family and I are, naturally, diehard Packers fans (Bears fans, please do not set fire to this book or destroy your smartphone or computers). While we were in Cancun, there was a Packers vs. Bears game being televised but we couldn't access it on the TV in our hotel room. I frantically called around to find somewhere to watch the game and the only place showing it was a chain restaurant with a reputation for great chicken wings and female servers in rather tight-fitting clothes. I had promised my six-year-old son we would see the game and, of course, no self-respecting Packers fan would miss a game against the Bears so I told my wife that my son and I were headed to a "local restaurant" to watch the big event.

No sooner had we settled in to enjoy the game, when my cell phone rang. It was a prospect I had been working with for months. I had been pitching Sales Sherpas to replace their incumbent advertising agency that wasn't getting results. Because of the game and the crowd there was a crazy amount of noise in the background. I told the prospect that I was sorry about the noise, and that it was "my son's birthday party," but I could take a few minutes for him. I'm happy to say that the Packers won that night and I landed the deal.

But the story is not over. I got back to the hotel and told my wife about the deal - Sales Sherpas biggest to date and one that would guarantee more financial security for my family - and, while she showed more relief than excitement, I understood that she was genuinely happy for me. Then I told my son to "tell mom about the Packers game." He exclaimed, "Well mommy, we went to this place to watch the Packers, and all these girls had really short shorts!" Let's just say that my wife's relief and happiness slightly tempered by disdain for my choice of venue.

Our family still jokes about that story to this day. When I reflect back, the elation I felt at closing that first, big deal and the lesson I learned about wearing so many hats when you're an entrepreneur are the ones I carry with me. You can't just focus on operations and product development and forget about sales. You must keep that sales pipeline full. I also realized that I couldn't do it all myself, and that I needed to be focusing on sales, and this new deal would require me to hire my first employee. As much as I didn't want to take the financial hit of putting someone on the payroll, I knew that it had to happen. It was time to start building a team.

It was painful to cut into my company's cash flow and take on overhead. Now, you are taking money out of your own pocket, away from your family, to pay others. But, eventually, every growing business has to expand its human resources. One person simply can't do it all. I hired my first employee,

Carol, to manage relationships with our copywriters, graphic designers and software developers and to conduct billing. I hired Carol because she had the ability to be friendly yet firm. I could leave the office for days on trips and know that everything was handled, so I could focus on growing the company.

Startup Insight: Eventually you will get to the point where you need to acknowledge you can't do it all. You need to go out, make that first hire, and stay focused on growing the business.

Tips on Selecting your First Team Members

It is easy to fall into the trap of hiring friends or people just like ourselves, or as HR professionals call it, the "me too effect." We like to talk with people with similar work experiences, backgrounds and communication styles. So, the natural inclination is to hire those people.

In specific functional areas within traditional corporations you will find groups of people with similar skills and, frequently, similar communication styles. For example, in accounting departments, you tend to get highly analytical people that take the time to prepare thoughtful answers to difficult questions, but they sometimes suffer from "paralysis through analysis." In sales departments, you tend to get highly driven, goal-oriented people who usually are not known for their detail orientation. But you have your VPs, directors and C-Level teams that coordinate each of those functional areas and theoretically, steer the ship in the right direction.

It is not natural to spend time thinking about your weaknesses or gaps in competencies (knowledge, skills and abilities) relative to the other functional areas.

The startup world tends to have a way of quickly making you self-aware of those weaknesses. If you are an accounting or finance major, you might focus on building out your cash flow projections, planning on how to get funding for your startup, etc. If you are a marketing major, you might focus on creating your marketing plan, building out your website or creating your social media presence. If you are an engineering major, you might start creating your project plan or building a prototype. If you are a CS (computer science) major, you might start writing code and creating a roadmap.

However, suddenly, if you are an army of one, you have to do all of this! Eventually, you realize that it is impossible to do it all yourself, and that you need to identify your own strengths and weaknesses relative to the MOST CRITICAL NEEDS OF THE STARTUP. You can't just hire people at will; you probably have little to no money. You need to ask yourself what gaps need to be filled that will help the startup survive and thrive. If you invest this dollar today in this employee, will you start getting it back tomorrow, next week, next month?

Startup Culture

There is a common misconception that startup founders shouldn't dedicate their time to thinking about culture.

Aaron Everson shared some great insights relative to his experiences at Jellyfish and Shoutlet.

"When you are starting out, you have to find people who are super passionate. They need to want to put in the extra time and energy that many times isn't required in a regular job. Having the qualifications to do the job is simply not enough. When I am interviewing employees at one of my startups, I ask myself, could I spend all day in a room with this person? If I can't, they are not a good fit.

We spent a great deal of time thinking about culture at Shoutlet. Not just the current culture, but the future culture as well. We looked at things as basic as the paint on the walls. We chose colors that were fun and uplifting. I remember an employee who came up to me one day and said, "I love it here, I don't think I could ever leave." That's the point.

The other thing I find is that it takes conscious effort to define and live a new culture. However, over time it starts to take on a life of its own. One of our employees created a Facebook page called Overheard. It was completely unplanned. The purpose was to share all the funny things that people said at the office. The next thing you know, people were just bursting out laughing randomly during the day. It was great; it reinforced our culture of fun."

Startup Insight: Define your culture when you start your company. Hire people you know will live that culture, then watch it manage itself.

Hire Slowly, Fire Quickly

If you want to learn the real importance of the old adage "hire slowly and fire quickly," launch a startup. The temptation is not to plan ahead and to wait until the last minute to hire someone, simply because the cash does not exist to hire all the team members you require. Then, you make a hire out of desperation to fix a problem (e.g. increase sales, launch your software for those beta users). The best-case scenario is that you have a really good picture of their skill sets, they match your needs, perhaps they were referred to you or you worked with them (but they have a strong appreciation for the startup roller coaster ride) and they "hit the ground running."

It is rare that all of these stars align. More often than not, startups don't have the luxury of having a classic 60- to 90-day hiring cycle (from job posting all the way to an employee's start date). You might have a week or even a few days. So, you hire someone who is unproven, and you don't think about how you will actually get along with this person. You essentially have just married someone after a one-hour first date.

Problems then start to bubble up ... the person might miss a critical deadline, they might come into work late, you find out they don't have the skills they professed during the interview, or you find that you just don't like them as a person. But you decide to gut it out. You don't have the money or time to find someone else. You tell yourself things like, "they will get better," "we will learn to get along."

Before you know it, critical deadlines are missed and your beta gets delayed, or your product doesn't function at all. You find out you have no truly qualified sales leads, you start yelling at each other and you are hemorrhaging cash. You tell the person to "get the hell out—you're fired."

But, it isn't that simple. You told them you would give them a 10 percent equity stake in the company. Perhaps they are the only one with access to the code (and the only Java you understand is the delicious elixir that gets you rolling every morning at 6 a.m.), they didn't give you the login credentials to your CRM (customer relationship management software with all of your sales leads) and they tell you they are going to work for your large, well-funded competitor.

I spoke with Brian Taffora, managing director of venture capital firm, CSA Partners. CSA Partners invests in early-stage, high-growth companies. We discussed traps that founders can fall into when hiring the first group of employees and ways to avoid those traps.

"We find situations where there might be a founding team of three or four people, and we provide them funding. As soon as they have the money, they immediately think, alright, we have to hire right away. They simply look around, say "who do we know that we can hire," and they automatically hire them without thinking and analyzing what they really need. Before you know it, their burn is out of control, they have employees who are not qualified, and they cannot attach an ROI to each person. Things spiral out of control.

The other classic situation I see with startups hiring too quickly is that they haven't thought through the process that these new employees need to follow. The founders have created a solid business model, they are experiencing rapid customer adoption, and revenue growth is also accelerating. They now have the capital they were seeking, so the founder(s) steps outside of that sales role without defining and refining their sales process.

For example, the new salespeople don't know the product, they don't understand the sales process, they aren't prepared for customer objections and then everything falls apart. We actually had a situation like this occur with one of our portfolio companies. The company closed on their A round with us. They quickly grew their salesforce to 24 people. Because there was no process, and they were not being carefully managed, it created a toxic mess. The company ended up firing 14 people, obviously getting down to 10 people, tightened up their processes, and sales actually increased from when they had 24 people.

It is really critical to define and refine your processes and take the time to hire the right people before you grow your team.

Lastly, it is critical that founding team members share the company culture with new hires so those new hires understand why the company is in business, who their customers are and how the company makes money. Without that understanding, a company will never reach its goals."

I haven't met anyone in my career who likes to fire people. I know people who had it down to a science, where it was simply a process of their job, like that of any other job. I used to have a director of HR at a Fortune 500 company who was a genuinely great guy and mentor to me. He was very process oriented. We followed the classic corporate "four coaching sessions/write-ups and then you are out" process. But if there had been an obvious hiring mistake and that mistake became quickly apparent, he would have no hesitation telling the manager to fire the person right away.

There was no point in hoping the person's behavior would improve or that they would magically learn the skills they said they possessed during the interview. One of the things the guy used to do when he had to fire someone in a high-profile role was to wear all black. Imagine Johnny Cash in an HR department. Whenever we saw him come into the office in black, we knew some bad stuff was going down and steered clear of him. In the end, it became a running joke in the office.

Startup Insight: When it becomes apparent the person isn't going to work out, you need to get rid of them right away. Startups don't have the luxury of time or money needed to keep someone on who doesn't contribute immediate value to helping the startup survive and thrive.

Creating a launch plan (more on that later) and anticipating your needs can help mitigate some of the aforementioned nightmare scenarios for entrepreneurs. Start talking to your network, other entrepreneurs, angel investors and startup accelerators. Join startup groups and put the word out for people you will need well in advance of when you actually need to hire them.

Then, take the time to write a clear job description of the role. It not only helps the applicant to understand some of the expectations, but helps you clarify what you need in that person. It also creates a professional image of your firm and makes it easier to recruit. It is critical that you also make it 100 percent clear they will be wearing many hats, and if they aren't comfortable with that, they shouldn't work for your startup (perhaps recommending your competitor). Startup job descriptions need to be very results oriented. You need to set clear expectations coming in and not have job descriptions filled with fluff that doesn't drive immediate results in order to move your startup forward.

On the next page is an example of a job description from one of my startups for a business development manager (sales) role:

Business Development Manager – Role Description

Role Summary:

The business development manager will be part of a dynamic startup company and be responsible for growing and supporting the business.

Responsibilities:

- Become an expert at identifying challenges prospects face, which can be solved with our software solution.
- Generate highly qualified lead opportunities.
- Identify critical influencers and decision-makers within prospect organizations.
- Qualify prospective small and medium business leads.
- Close new business consistently at or above quota level.
- Follow up on inbound and outbound leads.
- Develop marketing, web and other advertising initiatives.
- Work collaboratively with other marketing team members and software development to execute a sales strategy.
- Work with team members to constantly refine the company's business model to maximize company growth.
- Other responsibilities ... this is a startup, so you need to be flexible.

Requirements:

- Desire and ability to exceed measurable performance goals
- Demonstrated sales successes (preferred)
- Experience working in a startup environment (preferred)
- Demonstrated results of effective teamwork
- Energy, passion, sense of humor
- Superior written and verbal communication skills
- Strong organizational and time management skills

Independent Contractors

My business partner and I had gotten Bungee to a point where I was back to making a reasonable living, but I was still not making what I did in corporate. Although I was wearing many hats, my business partner, Troy, was focused on software development.

My responsibilities included marketing, attending trade shows, conducting sales calls, closing sales, creating marketing campaigns for my clients, managing copywriters, meeting with graphic designers, planning trade shows with Salesforce, preparing for investor meetings, following up on late payments, making deposits of client payments, and on and on.

I was working six days a week and sometimes seven. I was getting worn down. I wasn't spending much time with my kids; I was short when talking with my wife; I wasn't spending time with friends, and I wasn't making time for any of my personal escapes (in my house, these are known as the "3 Bs" – Biking, Boating and Brewing).

I spent Saturdays and sometimes Sundays doing non-revenue generating activity. You want to spend your "primetime" during the week (in the case of B2B), working with customers when they are available, including doing the books, processing payables (paying all the bills), logging all your receipts, dealing with taxes, running financial statements, etc. Not only did I despise this part of my startup life, but it was taking away what little time I had with my family. My children were 9 and 7 at the time, and I knew I needed to spend more time with them. I also wanted to get back to having "date nights" with my wife.

I spoke again with my first startup mentor and dear friend of mine, Joe Jeka. Joe had an extremely successful trade show company and retired early. He lives on a gorgeous spot on our lake. Joe knew I was worn down, and I asked him what I should do. His response was very direct: *"Dave, you are killing yourself, you have grown your business where it is cash flowing, but you are working on weekends doing the books, not spending time with your family, and not enjoying any of your hobbies. You have the money; go out and get yourself a bookkeeper."*

There wasn't enough work to justify a full-time bookkeeper on staff. So, I decided to go out and find a bookkeeper who would work as an independent contractor. I found Angie, who to this day does bookkeeping for one of my startups. I then simply set up QuickBooks online. I connected our business bank account to QuickBooks. Invoices went out electronically, then funds were paid back into QuickBooks and deposited into our bank account. She logs into the software anytime she needs to; so, does our accountant and so do I.

Why use Independent Contractors?

When you work for a company and you need to add another member to your team, you have a number of ways to fill that need. It's often as simple as just reaching out to your recruiting department and they'll find a person for you. You may review resumes at online job sites or reach out to local agencies. But you don't have that luxury you are a college student. The money to pay your team is coming out of your pocket. Not only do we need to be very careful to hire the right person, as we discussed previously, but you also need to know when to hire.

When I was a corporate manager we would just go out and hire employees. If an employee didn't perform to standard, most companies would require us to go through a classic performance improvement process which consisted of these steps: coaching session(s), first verbal warning, second verbal warning, written warning, then termination. Each step had to be meticulously recorded and kept in the employee's file. It's a long process, often taking many months - especially if an employee improves but then backslides.

Even when startups have the money to pay employees, they DON'T have the luxury of hiring the wrong person. Making the wrong hire can be fatal to a startup. Hire the wrong software developer, and you might not hit a deadline for that critical client. Hire the wrong business development manager and, if they don't hit their sales goals, they could cause you to burn through cash too quickly.

The answer? The independent contractor (sometimes just called a contractor or subcontractor, depending on circumstances).

A contractor is an independent individual or group of individuals who provide services to organizations on a project basis. These people are typically experts in their fields or have the ability to learn the skills necessary to complete a project or achieve a goal in short order.

The benefits of contractors to a startup are significant:

1. They tend to be very highly motivated (they only get paid when they deliver results).
2. You eliminate the need to take on long-term overhead.
3. You can quickly select them to do work.
4. You can quickly terminate them if they don't accomplish the work assigned.
5. You don't have to pay taxes or benefits.
6. You get the opportunity to see them complete their tasks under a microscope, and if they do a great job, you can offer them a job, thereby reducing the risk of hiring the wrong person.

Common Mistakes with Contractor Classifications

You need to be extremely careful when selecting someone as a contractor when, in fact, they should be classified as an "employee." Some businesses classify individuals as contractors when they should be employees in an effort to avoid paying taxes, workers compensation insurance, health insurance or other benefits.

In our currently exploding "gig economy," there are many companies accused of operating in a very grey area (e.g. Uber) regarding the people who are gigging for them. The question is whether their hires should be classified as an employee or a contractor. Attorneys are out to protect people who should be classified as employees, ensuring that they are paid appropriately and that they receive benefits. State Departments of Revenue and the IRS want to make sure that companies pay all of their required taxes.

Once a company starts dictating the hours someone can work, where they work, or if the company provides supplies and equipment, the workers are no longer "generally" deemed contractors, but employees.

Here are the three factors, directly from the IRS, on how to classify people as employees or contractors.

"Facts that provide evidence of the degree of control and independence fall into three categories:

1. **Behavioral**: Does the company control, or have the right to control, what the worker does and how the worker does his or her job?
2. **Financial**: Are the business aspects of the worker's job controlled by the payer (e.g. things like how the worker is paid, whether expenses are reimbursed, who provides tools/supplies, etc.)?
3. **Type of Relationship**: Are there written contracts or employee-type benefits (e.g. pension plans, insurance, vacation pay, etc.)? Will the relationship continue, and is the work performed a key aspect of the business?"

Source: Internal Revenue Service website, Oct 2017

Don't guess on whether you deem a person an independent contractor or an employee. You can end up with serious issues with your state and the federal government if you are not paying taxes for someone who should be classified as an employee. Talk with your accountant for guidance.

One of my startups selected an independent contractor, Lynn, to be an independent sales agent for us, not a business development person (salesperson). She was not on our payroll and was only paid based on commission. We did not tell her what hours she should work. She invoiced us for the commissions she had earned. She did not have a company computer, but would come into our office for weekly sales meetings.

One day we received a "friendly letter" from the Wisconsin Department of Revenue stating that they were conducting an audit into whether Lynn was actually serving as an "independent contractor" or an "employee." When you are busy running a startup, these are the last kind of issues you want to spend your time on, and frankly, they are stressful if you haven't experienced them before. I had been careful not to cross the line into what was deemed an employee, and we were fine—Lynn was, in fact, deemed to be an independent contractor. The headaches of the paperwork, phone calls and emails, however, were a major distraction. If you do step over the line, you will not only have to deal with this onslaught of distractions from your day-to-day business, but you will also face fines, payments for back taxes and be placed on a watch list for the future.

If you do select someone as a contractor, it is critical that you develop a contractor agreement. Two critical elements you must include are that the work is "for hire," and that they agree to a non-compete and non-disclosure clause. I have seen many startup founders have a contractor begin work without a contractor agreement. Then the relationship goes sour and the contractor might have proprietary information they could use to launch their own startup (your friendly, new competitor). Without an agreement, they could also imply you that intended to hire them as an employee, not a contractor.

Talk with your attorney about creating a contractor agreement for your startup.

Startup Insight: Independent contractors can be a very flexible way to get work accomplished by highly motivated individuals and organizations without taking on overhead. But, make sure you do not classify someone as an independent contractor who should be an employee.

STEP 10

Creating Your Launch Plan & Developing Your Beta

Step 10 – Creating Your Launch Plan & Developing Your Beta

I see "wantrepreneurs," an individual that has a startup idea, but never executes to turn the idea into a startup, all the time who don't commit the energy to create a launch plan. This can result in never getting to launch, launching too early, creating confusion amongst team members, aggravating new prospective customers, losing money or just wasting time.

Although your temptation is to "just get it out there and launch," resist that temptation and develop a well-conceived plan, it will increase the probability of your startup surviving and thriving. Try and find a mentor or other entrepreneur with successful startup experience to sanity check your launch plan.

Here are some tips to help you create your launch plan:

1. Have everyone on the team help create the launch plan. This will ensure you don't miss any steps, and that you get buy-in from everyone.
2. Work backward from your full commercial launch date (this is the date when you are rolling out to initial market—not your beta).
3. Move backward to your beta date.
4. Make sure you allow double the amount of time you think you need to make product/service modifications based on feedback you receive from your beta.
5. Double to triple the amount of time you think you will need for product development (unless you have been through this process with similar products/services).
6. Clearly define the goals of your beta (what do you need to learn?).
7. Hold yourself and others accountable for deliverables and dates. Many of your tasks will be critical path (sequential stages that need to occur in order to achieve your goal).

8. Keep the launch plan dynamic and accessible online with a service such as Trello.

Basic Startup Launch Plan:

	01/01/18	02/01/18	03/01/18	04/01/18	05/01/18	06/01/18	06/15/18	07/01/18
Major Milestones								
Beta Launch					TODD			
Beta End						TODD		
Full Commercial Launch								TODD
Software Development								
Launch Beta Sign-Up Page	BILL							
Build User Interface (UI)		BILL	BILL	BILL	BILL			
Make UI Changes Based on Beta Results						BILL	BILL	
Back-End Development		JENNY	JENNY	JENNY	JENNY			
Make Back-End Developed Changes Based on Beta Results						JENNY	JENNY	
Usability Testing							JENNY	
Beta Live								BILL

Sales & Marketing

Task								
Telesales Calls to Prospective Customers	FRED	FRED	FRED	FRED	FRED	FRED		
Weekly Website Traffic Analysis (Begins Post Website Home Page Launch)		JOHN	JOHN	JOHN	JOHN	JOHN	DM	
Develop Intro Video		ANNA						
Search Optimize the Website				MARY				
Set-up Marketing Automation Software				MARY				
Promote Videos on Social Media			LYNN	LYNN	LYNN	LYNN		
Recruit DBD (Director of Business Development)		JOHN	JOHN	JOHN	JOHN	JOHN		
Weekly Webinars with Prospects							DBD	
Recruit DM (Director of Marketing)								
Paid Search Campaigns				TODD	TODD			
Tradeshow Management						DM	DM	DM
On-going Sales Efforts						DBD	DBD	DBD
On-going Marketing Efforts						DM	DM	DM

Legal

Task								
File for LLC	TOM							
Create Operating Agreement	TOM	TOM						
Create Terms and Conditions				TOM	TOM			
Create Privacy Policy			TOM					

Finance

Register for Federal Tax ID		TOM						
Open Bank Account			TOM					

Client Support

Conduct Beta Planning Meetings				TEAM	TEAM			
Develop Training Materials (Based on Learning from Meetings)				JENNY	JENNY			
Set-up 800 Number and Integrated Chat				BILL				
Provide Tech Support (on-going)							JENNY/ BILL	JENNY/ BILL

Designing an Effective Beta

Pilot testing is when a select group of end users tries the system under an initial test, before deployment, to provide feedback about the product.

Beta testing is done at the client side (last stages of development cycle), where all end users use the system to see whether the system is working as per their given requirements.

Many startups do not differentiate between the two, using the terms interchangeably. Frequently, due to demands on time, they are both conducted at the same time. We are going to be focusing on conducting betas.

Before we specify the objectives of the beta, it is important to determine who the people are that need to be engaged in the beta.

Tips on selecting your beta target market

1. Ensure the market is representative of your target market.
2. Select a sample size that is large enough to gather necessary feedback.
3. Provide enough time to gather feedback.
4. Choose a market that cannot be easily impacted (positively or negatively) by outside sources (e.g. competitors, biases from your startup, non-representative economic factors, etc.).
5. Select a target market you can rely on to provide you with timely feedback (I would recommend coordinating a minimum of weekly meetings/calls/webinars).

When designing your beta, it is critical to define the specific objectives you need to achieve.

Sample Beta Objectives:

1. **Customer usability** - What modifications do you need to make so customers can easily navigate and gain the proposed benefit of your software? What additional details are needed in the instructions?
2. **Product quality** - Does your product survive rigorous usage by customers?
3. **Feature set** - What additional features does your product/service need?
4. **Marketing** - Does your marketing effectively describe the features, functionality and benefits?
5. **Channels** - Where do your customers want to purchase your product?
6. **Pricing** - How much are customers willing to pay you for your product/service?
7. **Customer service** - How do customers want to receive customer support? Are they willing to pay additional fees for additional support? This is common in the B2B software market.
8. **Competitive advantages** - How does your product/service compare to other products/services they have used? Are there any weaknesses that need to be addressed? Are there any competitive strengths that need to be accentuated in your marketing?
9. **Satisfaction** - What was their overall satisfaction with the product or service?
10. **Future** - Would they like to participate in future betas? Would they like to be contacted for purchase when you roll out commercially?

Determining the Beta Length

Simply put, the length of the beta must be long enough to gather all of the insights needed to modify the business model. We typically see betas running 4-8 weeks. However, the level of product complexity and demands of the startup frequently flex that range.

The Art of Setting Low Expectations

Our natural inclination as entrepreneurs is to be eternally optimistic, even delusionally optimistic, as we discussed before. However, when that optimism turns into setting high customer, employee and investor expectations, we can set ourselves up for failure. I tend to take the opposite approach and set expectations incredibly low. It reduces the self-imposed stress on you and your startup.

I will set expectations low when rolling out a beta with statements such as this:

"We appreciate you taking the time to participate in our beta. Please remember it is beta, and the purpose is for us to receive your feedback and modify our product/service accordingly. It is important for you and all those participating to know there will be problems/confusion. Our goal will be to fix those problems and address that confusion during the beta, but that will not always be possible."

Creating a Feedback Loop

Given that you are requesting time, energy and potentially money from prospective customers to beta your product or service, it is important that you have a process in place to respond to their feedback in a timely manner (even if you can't make modifications based on that feedback during the course of the beta). Without this feedback loop, critical insights that you need to gather from your beta can be lost, which can have catastrophic implications if you roll out and your product/service does not operate as your startup had promised.

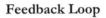

Feedback Loop

My recommendation is to have frequent meetings, webinars or calls with beta users to review participant feedback. At a minimum, provide an interactive way for beta participants to provide feedback. Frequently, they will have a great number of details to share, and you may have follow-up questions.

I am going old school here and recommend you provide your beta participants your phone number [gasp]. Beta participants are not going to want to spend the time taking screen captures, marking them up and providing written descriptions of the problem in an email or feedback form.

If you make the process difficult for them, they will simply not provide you feedback or not enough to ensure you have the information you need to successfully modify your business model/product/service.

Startup Insight: Set low expectations for your beta customers. It will help the beta customers understand that things will go wrong and they will be pleasantly surprised if the problems are only minor. Setting expectations low also takes pressure off you and your team.

STEP 11

Cash Flowing Your Startup

Step 11 – Cash Flowing Your Startup

"Just keep spending until I say stop"

We have all heard the saying, "Cash is king." Individuals who have not launched startups rarely appreciate the critical nature of that statement. Cash is the lifeblood of a startup. Without cash, the startup frequently dies. This can be very different from the situation with your employer where employees sometimes spend company funds with blatant disregard for where the cash came from and no concern about where it will come from in the future.

When I was a marketing manager at a Fortune 500 firm (which will remain nameless) just beginning my first week of work, I was beginning to build out my marketing plan for the year. During the conversation with my marketing director about our sales objectives, I asked about the size of my budget. The response he gave me was, "Just keep spending until I say stop." I wisely watched my money. Unfortunately, others in my department didn't. They ran out of cash in the third quarter and I had enough budget for the entire year.

Established organizations typically have easy access to external sources of cash, including accessing lines of credit, selling stock, issuing bonds, selling inventory, etc. to fund operations with cash. Startups are very fragile. Typically, startups do not have the aforementioned relatively easy methods of raising cash. Entrepreneurs are spinning so many plates when formulating and refining their business model that it is very easy to take their eye off the available amount of cash—especially if that cash is blended with personal bank accounts. This is a frequent cause of startup demise. Don't let this happen to your startup. Keep a constant eye on your cash.

Make sure you create a separate bank account for your business to separate your finances for accounting and tax purposes. Mixing your business and personal finances, at best, creates confusion for your accountant and, at worst, will yield a visit from a friendly IRS agent.

Startup Insight: Keep a constant eye on your available cash. Cash is the lifeblood of the startup.

Cash Flow Management 101

For a great crash course on cash flow management, I turned to my colleague, Tim Carr. Previously, he served as a director at Robert Baird, a wealth management and private equity firm. He has also founded multiple startups of his own. Tim earned his MBA in Finance from the University of Chicago, and now teaches in the Finance Department at the University of Wisconsin-Whitewater, in addition to mentoring startups.

Here is Tim's crash course for you:

Cash Flow Traps:

1. How will you fund your new business?
2. Is your startup funding sufficient?
3. Is your startup funding too much?
4. Will your cash flow support your business?
5. Are your sales estimates, right?
6. Are accounts receivable and accounts payable causing your cash crunch?

How will You Fund Your New Business?

Many new entrepreneurs have stars in their eyes thinking about their "great idea." It is going to be amazing. They are thinking it is exactly what is needed. They get the business formed, start getting things moving forward, and then it hits them. How am I going to capitalize it? Where will I get funding? I've worked a while and have saved up money, but do I really want to risk it all on a startup?

That is exactly what most businesses do.

According to the Kauffman Foundation, 86 percent of new businesses are started with personal savings. Out of that, 16 percent with credit cards, 8.5 percent with retirement funds, and 6.5 percent with home equity or bank loans.

Jeff Bezos started Amazon with $10,000 before getting money from each of his parents, which is usually the second place for funding after the founders or co-founders. He then got funding from friends, more family members, acquaintances, then venture capital and an IPO. All of that happened in roughly three years. You could only hope for such skyrocketing moves. This is not the norm. In fact, only 0.1 percent of all startups in 2015 received venture capital funding according to KPMG. This means you need to plan as though this kind of move will never happen, because it probably won't, but you can be very successful if you plan right.

Startup Insight: Have a self-funding plan. Don't make your startup's success contingent on raising outside capital (e.g. angel investors).

Is Your Startup Funding Sufficient?

You know what options are available to you to start your new business, but you don't have enough cash in the bank to get through the first six months of operations, let alone the first couple of years. This can cause you to go into desperation mode. Do you save your business by borrowing from anyone you can, or just let it die? You are so worried about the financial side of the business that the actual business starts to stagnate or falter.

Depending on the type of business you are going into, your startup funding can differ significantly. If you are setting up a retail store, you have to consider the time to remodel or do a buildout, if needed. You also need to consider the time necessary for customers to find you, to acquire repeat customers, and to reach cash flow to stabilize above break even while paying yourself, not just your other employees. Many new entrepreneurs look at the business side and project out their revenues and costs, but when the topic of getting a salary comes up they say "once we are profitable, I will take a salary."

Okay, that's fine, but you are living off of savings in the meantime and you're starting your business with savings as well. This is not sustainable for the long term. Always include a salary for yourself in your startup's financial projections. This will illustrate how much startup capital or savings is actually needed for the new venture. For retail, you should have at least six months of capital to get the business going although one year's worth would be ideal, to be safe.

If you are going into an area that is a bit more involved—like software design or biotech—you are going to have to go through the same process as above in determining how much you need to start your project. Again, remember to include your salary. If not taking one at first, ask yourself how you are going to live. You still need to sleep somewhere, eat and get around. At some point, you will need to get paid.

With these more capital-intensive industries, there will be a longer lead time. Oftentimes, three years or more. If looking at drug development, it takes much longer. You have Phase 1, 2 and 3 to get through. You don't need all of the funding Day 1 for these companies, though you need enough money to get to your next major milestone. You need enough of a cushion in case it takes you longer than you think to get there. When you get to that next milestone, various funding doors should start to open. This does lead you to your next cash flow problem: What if you get all the money needed Day 1?

Is Your Startup Funding Too Much?

Say you are a software company, and you have a big benefactor funding your startup. They give you $5 million and say go ahead, build it. Now, I know what you're thinking: This is perfect—we have all of the money needed for a long time to develop and program and test our software. This should be a no-brainer if the end product is any good. Right?

Unfortunately, more times than not, having too much money up front can cause almost as big of a problem as not having enough. The problem is that most new entrepreneurs don't budget properly or, if they did initially, they don't stick to that budget. They find a great office space and just have to have it. Why not, right? They have the money. Or they find an extremely talented programmer. Yeah, some of their skills overlap with existing team members, but they are fantastic, so they hire them. Those fantastic people usually come with a high cost. When your company gets to the point where it is advertising, you might ask yourself, why not spend additional money on it? No one will buy our product if they don't know about us. You advertise like crazy—even if it blows the budget. Every expense that a business has should be looked at through the lens of, "is it necessary right now?" Will it help us move forward? Does the cost outweigh the benefit?

Going back to the advertising example, most products or services take at least five interactions of some kind before the consumer will buy it. That number goes up as the cost and complexity of the product increases. It also goes up when the time frame is shortened. That means having five ads hit you today probably won't make you buy it if you don't hear about it again for a month. Each interaction has a declining marginal impact in the short run.

Services like advertising can be contracted out. Especially at first, this is a good idea to keep costs down while having a professional guide you through the process, as mentioned in an earlier topic. Be careful, though; you don't want to contract out the necessary components of your business. It can change your business's dynamics and that individual's personal motivations.

You have the money to start the business. You understand the length of time before traction will occur, but...

Will Your Cash Flow Support Your Business?

Determining your cash flow starts with your projections. How do you think your business will do? How quickly will customers buy your product/service? Will they come back and buy more?

The first step in this process is asking...

Are Your Sales Estimates Right?

First, you need to break down who your customers are. How long will it take them to find you or try your product? How often will they purchase? Are there seasonal variations to their purchases, like buying more in the summer than the winter, like a swimsuit? Are there cyclical variations or some other timing involved in the purchase? For example, a subscription service that lasts a year or two. Where are you selling? Locally, regionally, or worldwide? Will everyone want your product, or is it based on some other demographic, like male vs. female or older vs. younger?

As you work through these questions, and any others you think of that might be relevant for your particular product/service, you will get a breakdown of your sales profile. Once you have a profile of your customer, you can determine the size of the market you will be entering. Then you can determine the overall percentage of that market you hope to get. How long will it take to get there? What will be the ramp up in sales? Be realistic.

Once you have the size of the overall market and a roadmap for sales progression, you should have demand figures by month and year going forward. Depending on the type of company you are starting, the length of your forecast will change. Traditionally, you would put together three- to five-year projections. If you are creating something with a longer ramp up, you would want to have longer projections. Obviously, the longer the time frame you use, your ability to actually predict results will diminish, sometimes significantly. That's why the initial projection is just the beginning. As your business is progressing, you would compare actual results to your projected or budgeted figures and see what variances have occurred. You would then adjust accordingly, if it made sense to do so. If there was a one-time item present that caused your projections to be off by a lot, it doesn't make sense to adjust for it happening again. More on this later.

You've come up with sales estimates going out three years. You're done right? Sort of. How confident are you in those estimates? Sixty percent sure? What about the other 40 percent? Is there a 20 percent probability that you will generate that customer revenue much later in the year? Is there a 10 percent chance that sales don't ramp up this year at all? Is there a 10 percent chance that sales explode? If your answer is yes, then you should adjust your projections based on a change in demand for your product. This sensitivity analysis will allow you to average all of the different probabilities to your base case scenario and come up with a "best guess" for what your sales will look like.

It isn't as difficult as it sounds. Let's look at an example. Imagine you believe that you will sell 1,000 units in June.

	Base Case	Later in the year	Not at all this year	Sales explode
Probability	60%	20%	10%	10%
Units sold	1000	500	0	1700
(.6x1000) + (.2x500) + (.1x0) + (.1x1700) = 870 units				

When we average these together, we get a best guess of 870 units this year. A little bit more conservative than our 1,000-unit base case estimate, but more realistic, given the uncertainty of our startup.

This gets us back to whether your cash flow will support your business. You have your revenue picture from your sales and customer estimates. You now have to look at your expenses. You first need to put your expenses into two lists—must-haves and like-to-haves. The must-haves are things you cannot do without (think rent, build out—if needed, utilities, employees, office supplies, etc.). Get as detailed as you can. The more detail you have, the easier it will be to find spending issues later on. Like-to-haves might also include rent if you start by working out of your home, but would prefer an office. A certain employee might be a like-to-have because they are very talented, but also expensive. Once you've determined your must-haves list, estimate what the cost is for each item. You should concentrate on what actually drives the cost. Is it sales, number of customers, number of employees, number of locations, something else? This will allow you to estimate the cost per $1 or the cost per one unit sold of a product. It will also assist you in estimating the projected cost increases along with sales.

Don't forget taxes—once you are making money, that is. You know the government won't forget either. If you are setting up your business with property or machinery, depreciation will come into account, and so on. Although not a complete list of expenses, this gives you a basic outline of where to start.

You've put together your expenses and the drivers that increase or decrease them. This gives you your variable revenues and expenses along with your fixed components. You should list them accordingly on your spreadsheet, then take a second step on your income statement by subtracting them from your revenues.

You should now be looking at your net income projections on a monthly and yearly basis. How do they look? If you are like most startups, you will be losing money for a period of time before sales start to accelerate and then, hopefully, you will be making money. If your projections show you losing money, even after sales are accelerating, see if you made a mistake with data entry. If you didn't, then determine why you aren't. Are costs just too high? If that's the case, can you decrease the costs somehow, or is the venture just not viable? This is an extremely important question to ask. Don't let ego stand in your way. If you determine it isn't viable, it could be the best decision you ever made. A venture is only right if the numbers say it's right. Your personal biases should not cloud your judgement.

Assuming the numbers support you, going into business, at what point does it show you making money? When does it show you making money while paying yourself a salary? If this is six months in, make sure you have enough cash on hand for nine months to a year just to be safe. If it is two years, make sure you have enough cash on hand for three years. The farther in the future your breakeven point, the higher the probability that you can miss by a significant time frame. You want to make sure you don't run into a cash crunch just because things were pushed back by six months or so. As mentioned before, you must remember to consider paying yourself. You will need to survive, so make sure you personally have enough resources on hand to get through the time period, and not by eating rice cakes and ramen.

Are Accounts Receivable and Accounts Payable Causing Your Cash Crunch?

You have your income statement. You have a good idea about when you will break even. Are there other things to be looking out for? If you have an existing business and experience a bit of a cash crunch at various times, you should check your accounts receivable. A cash crunch occurs when you unexpectedly become short of cash, and accounts receivable are the amounts customers owe to you. They've already bought your good or service, but haven't yet paid you, which happens from time to time. Let's say most customers pay their bill within 30 days. Well, you start to plan that customers pay within 30 days and you also plan to have enough cash on hand to account for that. What if a customer stretches that to 60 days? How about 90 days? Do you have enough cash on hand for that to occur? Calculating the average number of days that customers take to pay their bills (accounts receivable turnover) can help you get a historical perspective and allow you to project whether customers are stretching to pay you.

If looked at on a monthly, semiannual and yearly basis, you can determine if there is any seasonality to it. You may not view your company as being seasonal in nature, but if your customers or their customers are more seasonal, they may pay you more quickly when cash flow is good, but stretch it out a bit when their cash flow is tighter. It is something to be aware of in running your business. For your cash flow statement, as the balance in your accounts receivable account is increased from month to month, it appears as if you are using cash, resulting in a negative flow on your statement. It makes sense. You sold your product or service, experienced expenses, and received the equivalent of an IOU. Remember to bill soon after delivering your product/service and aggressively pursue payments to keep accounts receivables in check.

Related to that is accounts payable. Accounts payable is what you owe to other people and haven't paid yet. You have permission to pay within 30 days, but, for right now, it shows up on your balance sheet as owing money to someone. This also makes sense. It is also a pseudo loan. Other companies are letting you buy their product/service, and they are also letting you wait to pay. They are basically loaning you money for that time period. If you stretch out paying them, thus making your accounts payable balance increase, you are effectively taking out a bigger loan for a period of time. This is kind of like a line of credit. From a cash flow perspective, this acts as a positive cash flow, because you are buying more goods or services and not paying for them … yet. In this process, you don't want to stretch payments out too far, as you do want to enjoy the favorable terms your vendor is giving you. (Example: One may give a 5 percent discount if you pay within 10 days.) You don't want them to force immediate payment on every purchase. Accounts payable does give you a little flexibility, though, in dealing with your cash flow.

By taking both accounts receivable and accounts payable into consideration, you have an interrelationship that affects your cash flow. If either one is moving in the wrong direction at any time, your cash flow could be affected.

You need to plan for the monthly fluctuations with a cash cushion and knowing how much is needed is key. That's why looking at specific categories and customers is so important.

One last way that I like to represent the impact of running out of cash is with the following graphic (Source Forbes). The graphic displays what is called "The Valley of Death" in the life of a startup. Obviously, the implication with "Death" is that the startup no longer has any cash and no additional sources of investment, which leads to the end of the startup's life.

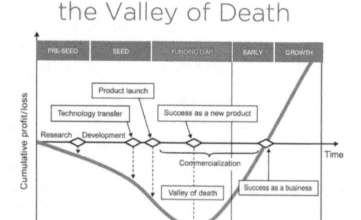

Cash Flow ... In Summary

We've looked at a number of things regarding your business's initial funding and cash flow. These are not static documents that we've created; they are living, changing things. They need to be compared to actual results and updated based on changes that are occurring in your business and industry. Your company's cash flow should be looked at daily and compared to projections and budgets at least monthly. This will allow you to stay on top of anything positively or negatively affecting your company's operations. It shouldn't take you very long if they are updated regularly and routinely. Meanwhile, it will ensure your company stays on firm footing, so you can minimize the probability of any cash crunches and keep cash flowing.

Payment Priorities Revisited:

When startups become desperate for cash, and there are no other funding sources besides personal savings, the stress levels in your family can become stratospheric.

I was in a cash crunch with my first startup, Sales Sherpas, during the second year of operation. I had paid our taxes, had to move an employee from full-time pay to part-time pay, negotiated an extra 60 days to pay our office rent and negotiated some advance payments on new client projects. However, even all of that led to me not bringing in a paycheck for my family for six months. I went weeks without a good night's sleep. It created a great deal of stress on my relationship with my wife and strain on my family—not just financially, but psychologically as well.

Fortunately, my wife and I had put a plan in place where we could live on her income, although things would be very tight. We stopped making payments into our kids' college funds, stopped taking our two annual vacations, minimized meals out, and when we did go out with friends (who had traditional jobs), I would suggest less expensive restaurants or just order a pizza or Chinese takeout. Eventually, the company started generating cash and the financial cloud was lifted for me personally, but I promised myself to be more careful with company cash in the future.

I discussed payment priorities briefly before, but this is critically important to your family and startup, so we are going to revisit briefly with a little more detail.

Here are the payment priorities to help startups survive and thrive:

Priority #1: The government (for taxes and licenses) - The government does not take kindly to not receiving their revenue and can shut down your business. Don't pay them and your goose is cooked. Game over.

Priority #2: Your employees - Effective organizations live and die based on people. Pay your people. If times get tight, move them to part-time, or perhaps move them into contractor roles.

Priority #3: Your suppliers - You might have critical suppliers of materials. Perhaps you have to have an office space. I find that many startups overspend for office space. Starting at your home is an office choice, but there is a great deal to be said for the camaraderie of a startup incubator or other shared work space.

Priority #4: Yourself - That's right, bucko. Your paycheck will be driven by how well you and your startup are performing. Without paying all of the aforementioned parties, though, you won't stay in business.

Following those payment priorities might even be intuitive now. But actually, living by them is an entirely different proposition. Be prepared, because at some point, you will be faced with a difficult decision on who won't be getting paid or who will have to wait to get paid. At some point, that party will be you.

The pain of being paid last will quickly fade when your business thrives and you reap the benefits. Non-entrepreneurs will say how "lucky" you are. Only entrepreneurs understand the sacrifices that are made to create a living, breathing and thriving company. Hang on to that quiet confidence and just smile.

Startup Insight: When you are the entrepreneur, you get paid last.

STEP
12

Should I Stay or Should I Go

Step 12 – Should I Stay Or Should I Go?

The Clash was a punk rock band formed in 1976 in Britain, my birthplace, who went on to play throughout the 80s and were eventually inducted into the Rock and Roll Hall of Fame. One of the Clash's more famous songs was, "Should I Stay or Should I Go?" * I recommend you go to YouTube or other streaming music service and listen to the song before proceeding. You will be entertained and, more importantly, learn a good lesson.

Here are some of the most critical lyrics from

"Should I Stay or Should I Go?"

Should I stay or should I go now?
Should I stay or should I go now?
If I go, there will be trouble
And if I stay it will be double
So, come on and let me know
Should I stay or should I go?

* Clash. YouTube. The Clash. CBS Studios. 1977.

As I reflect on the best way to guide you through your life as a college entrepreneur, I want to address a controversial topic that could become very real for you. I will not take a position one way or the other, but I will lay out the facts for you. The topic is whether you should stay in school or leave, if you decide to focus 100% of your time on your startup.

I interviewed Anna Tracy, who founded Greet Feet, a branded footwear company, while in college. Anna began creating hand-painted shoes while in high school and sold $25,000 worth of shoes one pair at a time! She applied and was accepted into our Launch Pad startup accelerator. She eventually decided to scale her business and off-shored production. Then she went on to raise $50,000 in investment capital. Anna discussed the struggle she faced with whether to graduate or drop out of college and pursue her startup full time.

"Growing my startup while in college with a combined degree in graphic design and entrepreneurship was no easy task. It meant many long nights. I was juggling calls between investors and going to classes. Sometimes, I was managing logistics with China and taking exams and doing homework. I must have asked myself a thousand times whether I should drop out of school and work on Greet Feet full time … but at the end of the day, I knew that if the startup didn't reach my expectations, the odds of me going back to school were low and that I would always regret not getting my degree. So, I continued to juggle both and got my degree in Graphic Design and Entrepreneurship."

On the other hand, there are actually opportunities that encourage students to leave school in order to follow an entrepreneurial path, such as The Theil Fellowship, founded by Peter Theil. If you are not familiar with Peter Thiel, he is an entrepreneur, venture capitalist and philanthropist as well as one of the co-founders of PayPal and the first outside investor in Facebook.

The Thiel Fellowship, founded in 2011, is a two-year program for young people who want to build new things. Thiel Fellows who skip or drop out of college receive a $100,000 grant and support from the Thiel Foundation's network of founders, investors, and scientists.

As I mentioned previously, I am not going to include my opinion here. I am simply going to inform you of considerations, the pros and cons, and provide data, so you can make the best choice for yourself.

When this topic comes up with college-student entrepreneurs, the following college dropout examples always arise…

Bill Gates – Microsoft founder
Steve Jobs – Apple founder

Mark Zuckerberg – Facebook founder

Travis Kalanick – Uber founder

John Mackey – Whole Foods founder

The fact of the matter is, these entrepreneurs are the exception. Most people who leave college to focus on starting a business are, at best, moderately successful and, truthfully, many fail.

Let's address some of the pros and cons of leaving college and focusing 100 percent on your startup:

Pros of leaving college:

1. Focusing more time on your startup could lead to increased probability of success.
2. Leaving school will allow you opportunities to travel where and when you want to meet with customers, suppliers, team members, investors, etc.
3. Customers will take you more seriously if you are managing your startup full time.
4. Investors will take you more seriously if you are managing your startup full time.
5. You could start generating an income from the startup sooner.
6. You could get to market quicker with your product or service, thereby increasing the probability of success.

Cons of leaving college:

1. There is a strong chance you will not finish your degree; if you leave school, you will not return.
2. If you have student loans, you will need to begin paying them back immediately.
3. If you have grants, those funds will be lost.
4. If you shut down your startup, you are less likely to be employed. Students with some college but without a diploma have a 4%

unemployment rate vs. 2.5% for those with a bachelor's degree. (Source: Bureau of Labor Statistics).

5. You might disappoint family members, especially if they have invested money in your education.

6. Your lifetime earnings will probably be lower than if you finished your degree. The lifetime earnings of a person with some college courses but without a diploma is $1.73 million compared to the lifetime earnings of someone with a bachelor's degree: $2.31 million.

I think it is important to realize there are hybrid options as well. It's simply not as black and white as "should I stay or should I go."

Sam Lukach was a student of mine who, to date, generated more revenue before graduation than any other student. Sam launched a startup called Huk TV Mounts from his dorm room. His product helped students more efficiently use their dorm rooms with his patented TV mounting system. Sam eventually went from selling the Huk TV Mount hooks to college students through his eCommerce site and college bookstores to securing deals with a large provider of services within the healthcare sector. Sam went from roughly $25,000 in sales as a sophomore to $2 million by the time he graduated.

Here are his thoughts on staying or leaving college for your startup.

"The last year of school was very stressful. I had a thriving business but was also a full-time student. It was incredibly draining. The real decision was whether I should push my business to the next level, which would mean securing a $2 million deal and literally make me a millionaire, or focus on school and possibly risk losing the $2 million deal. The choice seemed pretty obvious to me: drop out of school and I could always come back. My parents were **not** enthusiastic about this choice and I also went and spoke with Gee. What I had not considered was a way to accomplish both. I worked with the university to go to part-time and finish in two semesters instead of going full-time my last semester (and took some classes online so I could travel to meet clients and my vendor in China). I am not going to kid you. It was a ton of work and extremely stressful.

But in the end, I landed the deal, my business became very successful, I finished my degree and yes, I did quite well financially. Before you make the decision to drop out, talk to your professors or department chairperson or the Dean of your college (if necessary) and see if there can be accommodations made. Remember, the university wants you to be successful and also graduate. You will find that they will probably be willing to work with you."

There are unconventional and rarely discussed ways to launch and grow your startup without dropping out of college but rather making modifications to your current situation.

1. Reduce your course load. (Example: Drop from 16 credits to 8 credits and extend your graduation one by semester). *
2. Finish your degree online either through your current college or another college.
3. Ask for college credit for some of the work you are doing on your startup. For example, see if your startup work can qualify for an internship or an independent study course.
4. Change your major to a degree you can finish more quickly.
5. Change from a double major to a single major.

Regardless of what decision you make, take your time making the decision. The decision to leave college should not be made hastily or when under duress. Don't let a customer, an investor or a co-founder make the decision for you. You need to make the decision that is best for you both personally and professionally and for THE LONG RUN.

I would be remiss if I didn't discuss what can happen to college students that launch startups in college but eventually decide to shut them down. Frankly, this is more common than not. However, the college-student entrepreneur world opens up in a way that traditional college students will never experience.

The Life of a Graduating College Entrepreneur (even when they don't continue with their startup).

It's true that old school companies sometimes (still) won't hire college students that have already launched a startup. The fear is that these young entrepreneurs will leave and start their own companies again. The probability of this is obviously higher than for those students that haven't launched startups. Most of the students that I work with have no interest in working with these old school companies because they've experienced the potential of starting their own business and they've seen their own ideas come to life.

BUT, the progressive companies, the ones that are growing at breakneck speed, where almost every day is exciting and frequently exhausting, are the ones hiring students that launched startups while in college. These companies realize that these college students know how to rapidly identify a problem, analyze market opportunity, develop creative solutions, test the solutions, determine if a sustainable competitive advantage can be achieved, and determine if there is a viable business model. Candidly, these are combined skills that most traditional employees don't acquire in a lifetime at regular, corporate jobs.

I have seen some recent examples with students of mine. Jake Smith got a one-way ticket to LA and sought out jobs at startups. As mentioned earlier, Jake ended up at the fastest growing startup of all time, Bird. Austin Beveridge recently packed up his car and, with his girlfriend, took a long trip to San Francisco through the Southwestern United States. Within one week of sending job applications to the companies he was interested in working for, he received interest from companies like LinkedIn and Facebook. In the end, he accepted a job with Bolt, which is currently one of the Top 10 Fastest Growing Companies in the U.S. (Inc, Aug 2018). These college-student entrepreneurs were in high demand at companies that value the kind of skills they developed from developing and launching their own startups.

A traditional work life is the one that most people choose – a steady paycheck, a predictable workweek, and, most often, pretty boring work. There's nothing wrong with choosing this life if risk is not for you. But, with big risks come big rewards – an exciting life, the road less traveled, experiences you might otherwise never get to have. When you start your own business, you control your own destiny and you learn so much through your successes and failures. Best of all, if you explore the world of entrepreneurship while in college, you experience the highs and lows with significantly less risk than once you're on your own.

In Conclusion

I truly hope you make the decision to pursue your entrepreneurial journey while in college. It is exhilarating and more fulfilling than any traditional job you could ever have. It is not an easy course. Nowhere else will you experience the kind of emotional roller coaster that a startup provides. You will have to manage your time with great care, like never before. You will also experience the challenges of less time for your personal relationships, financial stressors and trying to carve a path with them *through* an unfamiliar jungle.

Determine your true motivations. Define what success looks like to you. Identify your priorities of relationships, classes and startup before you begin your journey. Research all the resources available at your college, local startup accelerators, incubators and law schools.

Talk with prospective paying customers and seek the truth about your startup idea. Develop a sound business model. Create a brand that communicates your value proposition. Share your startup with the world. Seek out mentors and network with other entrepreneurs. When the workload becomes too much for you to handle, go seek additional team members or contractors. Ask yourself with every dollar you spend what you will get in return on that dollar.

Don't drop out of college before you analyze creative ways to stay in college and continue growing your startup, it can almost always be accomplished.. Whether you continue with your startup or not you will learn lessons beyond your wildest dreams. These lessons become extremely valuable to companies, to the point where you become very marketable, and frankly where you can get some of the most rewarding jobs at the most exciting companies in the world.

...and now it is time to get ready to enjoy the greatest time of your life.
— G

Learn free startup insights and keep up-to-date with his latest startup on LinkedIn: linkedin.com/in/davidrgee/

Appendix

Startup Readiness Assessment™

We have created a tool to help you determine how ready you are to launch your startup.

Possess industry experience		0 = < 5 years 1 = 6+ years
Startup in top 10 high-growth sectors*		0 = No, 1=Yes
Secured buy-in from your family		-1= No, 1=Yes
Completed Business Model Canvas		0 = No, 1=Yes
Conducted minimum of 100 discovery interviews		0 = No, 1=Yes
Created marketing plan		0 = No, 1=Yes
Completed launch plan		0 = No, 1=Yes
Possess immediate access to 12 months of cash		0 = No, 1=Yes
Confirmation of no non-compete, nor NDA issues		0 = No, 1=Yes
Confirmation of no patent or copyright violations		0 = No, 1=Yes
Have a team with required and complementary skills		0 = No, 1=Yes
Secured legal entity status		0 = No, 1=Yes
Attorney-generated contracts		0 = No, 1=Yes
Total Score:		

*Utilize latest Kauffman Industry Growth Report (see page 18 for most current report as of the publishing of this book).

So, how ready are you?

Startup Readiness Assessment™ Key

Now check how prepared you are and your relative startup risk. Note, that it is not possible to eliminate risk with a startup.

< 4   = Unprepared with Extreme Risk

5 – 8 = Limited Preparedness with Significant Risk

9 – 11 = Prepared with Moderate Risk

12 + = Very Prepared with Manageable Risk

Pitch Deck Example - Scanalytics

[Used with permission from Scanalytics Inc.]

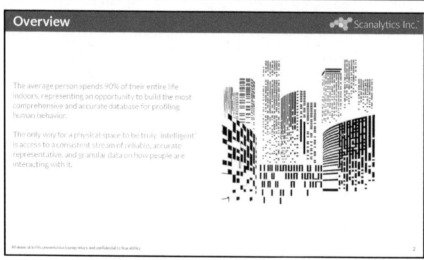

Scanalytics has created a solution that allows any building to constantly learn about its occupants. This layer of intelligence is then packaged as a stream of data by which applications can be created, effectively allowing us to build the "brain" for the built environment

Scanalytics Inc.

All material in this presentation is proprietary and confidential to Scanalytics   3

Traction   Scanalytics Inc.

We have built smart environments for customers like:

Powered by a team of scientists, engineers, and data experts, Scanalytics is the global leader in smart building sensor development and software platforms

Since founding, we have deployed thousands of sensors across multiple industry types including healthcare, retail, trade-show, and commercial office spaces

All material in this presentation is proprietary and confidential to Scanalytics   4

Market Opportunity

~ 100 billion sq feet of commercial space in United States alone

○ Energy efficiency
○ Occupant comfort
○ Operational efficiency

Representing annual spend to reach $102 billion by 2025

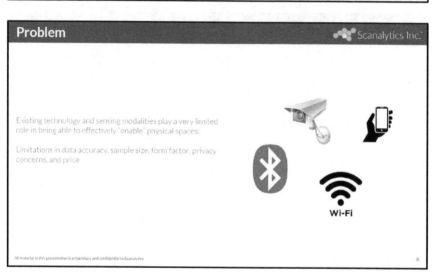

Problem

Existing technology and sensing modalities play a very limited role in being able to effectively "enable" physical spaces:

Limitations in data accuracy, sample size, form factor, privacy concerns, and price

Wi-Fi

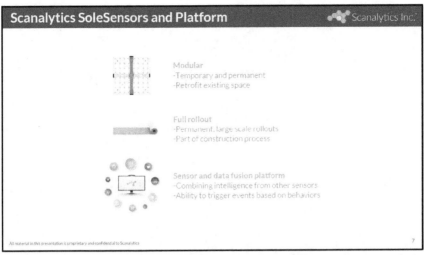

Scanalytics SoleSensors and Platform — Scanalytics Inc.

Modular
-Temporary and permanent
-Retrofit existing space

Full rollout
-Permanent, large scale rollouts
-Part of construction process

Sensor and data fusion platform
-Combining intelligence from other sensors
-Ability to trigger events based on behaviors

All material in this presentation is proprietary and confidential to Scanalytics

7

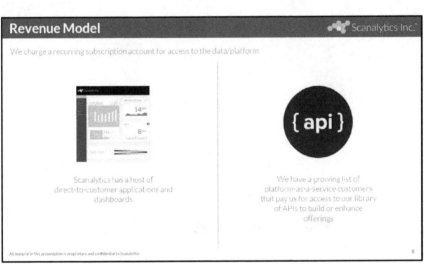

Revenue Model — Scanalytics Inc.

We charge a recurring subscription account for access to the data/platform

Scanalytics has a host of direct-to-customer applications and dashboards

{ api }

We have a growing list of platform-as-a-service customers that pay us for access to our library of APIs to build or enhance offerings

All material in this presentation is proprietary and confidential to Scanalytics

8

Marketing and Growth

Scanalytics leverages distribution and technology channel partners to acquire large enterprise customers at a lower cost.

We have VAR relationships with some of the largest flooring companies in the world, as well as leading technology companies like Intel, Microsoft, and Cisco

Team

 Scanalytics Inc.

Joe Scanlin - Cofounder/CEO

Experience in applied neuroscience, data analytics, and growing technology organizations

David Webber, PhD

Develops sensor fusion algorithms to transform raw data into meaningful information

Glossary - Terminology every entrepreneur must understand

Accelerator (or Startup Accelerator) - A formal program whereby entrepreneurs spend time with mentors who provide coaching, networking, financial investment and typically incubator space in return for a portion of equity in the startup. Accelerators typically receive 5-10 percent equity for their services upfront, sometimes with the option to purchase additional equity in the future.

Angel Investor (aka Angel) - An individual or group of individuals that invest money into startups, typically in exchange for equity. The easiest example to grasp is The Sharks on ABC's Shark Tank.

Acqui-hire - The acquisition of a company for the purposes of hiring their employees—not for the intrinsic value of the company.

Bootstrapping - The act of self-funding a startup. This can be funding that comes from the founder(s). Sometimes raising, friends/fools/family is considered bootstrapping.

Burn Rate (or "burn") - The rate at which a startup or company spends money. Typically measured per month. For example: If a company has a burn of $100,000 that would typically represent using $100,000 a month in cash. When burn rates increase at an unsustainable rate, investors can get nervous. The investors are left with a situation where they need the company to increase profits or investors need to put in more money to sustain the burn.

Business Model - The vision, mission and anticipated strategies related to product/service development, organization, legal, finance, sales, marketing and management of a startup.

Business Plan - A document that describes the business model in detail. Some investors will say that "business plans are dead or a waste of time; just create a pitch deck." However, this oversimplifies the value gained by asking difficult questions about how the startup will be organized, grown and managed.

C Corp - A corporate structure where its profits are taxed separately from its owners under sub step C of the Internal Revenue Code.

Company - A self-sustaining organization comprised of synergistic people and resources.

Convertible Note - Short-term loan made by investors that converts into equity based on an established milestone (e.g. valuation of the startup at a later funding round).

Copyright - Legal right of ownership of original work, used to protect literary works, live performances, photographs, movies and software (although rarely used for software).

Cost of Acquisition (CAC) - Generally calculated as the total cost that reflects the marketing and sales costs divided by the number of new customers over a given period of time. At the beginning of the startup lifecycle, these costs are typically very high due to significant sales and marketing costs relative to new customers acquired.

Crowdfunding - Crowdfunding is the process of raising capital to fund a startup, product, invention, project, literary work, event or special cause. This is usually done through a web-based campaign on a specific crowdfunding platform. There are four types of crowdfunding platforms: Reward Crowdfunding, Equity Crowdfunding, Donation Crowdfunding and Debt Crowdfunding.

Customer - (I know it might seem like I am insulting your intelligence here; instead, I am helping you avoid a frequent mistake made by new entrepreneurs.) An individual or group that PAYS you money for your product or services. Don't confuse a customer with a user of your product or service.

Early State Company - A startup that has matured to the point when market validation has been achieved, but process improvement and team expansion are required for the company to scale.

Entrepreneur - An individual who is the founder and manager of a startup.

Equity - The amount of ownership, typically represented as a percentage, that an individual or organization owns in a startup or other firm.

Exit - The sale of an organization for, ideally, a significant amount of cash or equity in another company. This is why individuals such as angels and VCs give you money. They need a return on their investment, just like you do on your investments. The other form of exit is shutting down the company.

Gig Economy - An economy where growth is driven by the use of independent contractors vs. traditional employees. Example: Uber's drivers are classified as contractors and help contribute to the "gig economy."

Incubator - A physical space with areas to collaborate where entrepreneurs congregate and manage their startups. Sometimes people confuse accelerators with incubators. Accelerators are programs, incubators are places. Frequently, accelerators can be located in incubators. For example: TechStars in Chicago is located in the 1871 incubator.

Intellectual Property (IP) - Refers to ideas, including inventions, music and literature. IP falls into two categories:

- Industrial Property includes patents for inventions, industrial designs for products and processes.
- Copyrights are legal rights of ownership to original work, used to protect literary works, live performances, photographs, movies and software (although rarely used for software).

Friends, Fools and Family (The 3 Fs) - Three external sources of investment capital available to many first-time entrepreneurs. Less than one percent of startups receive venture capital, so The 3 Fs are frequently used as a source of initial capital.

Limited Liability Company (LLC) - A corporate structure whereby the members of the company cannot be held personally liable for the company's debts or responsibilities. Limited liability companies are considered a hybrid between corporations and sole proprietorships.

Minimum Viable Product (MVP) - Most basic feature set in a product or service to determine if your value proposition resonates with prospective customers. A big trap first-time entrepreneurs fall into is adding features and functionality that are not required and convoluting the insights that need to be acquired.

Monthly Recurring Revenue (MRR) - Represents the measure of monthly revenue for service providers and typically Software-as-a-Service (SaaS) providers.

Non-Compete Agreement (Non-Compete) - Agreement between two parties (e.g. employee and employer) whereby one party (e.g. employee) agrees not to work for or create an entity that competes with the other party (e.g. the previous employer).

Non-Disclosure Agreement (NDA) - Agreement between two parties whereby "the disclosing party" provides proprietary information to "the receiving party" and restricts the sharing of the proprietary information with third parties. Don't ask angel investors to sign NDAs—they won't, and you will lose credibility.

Operating Agreement - An agreement between the members of a Limited Liability Company (LLC) that governs the business, including member powers, rights, duties and obligations. It also outlines the decision-making process related to operational, functional and financial issues in a structured manner. The operating agreement of LLC companies is similar to bylaws used by corporations.

Pitch - A brief presentation, typically under twenty minutes, whereby entrepreneurs present a rapid overview of their business model to prospective investors or other interested parties.

Pitch Deck - A series of electronic slides, usually under twenty, that displays the elements of a business model.

Pro Forma - Forward-looking financial documents, such as cash flow statements, based on hypothetical conditions.

Runway - How long, usually measured in months, a startup has before it runs out of cash.

Software as a Service (SaaS) - Software that is provided as an ongoing service, as opposed to a traditional initial outlay to purchase a software package. This pricing model is particularly appealing to small- and medium-sized businesses (SMBs) that don't traditionally have the budget to make large software purchases. SaaS companies have particular appeal to angel investors and venture capital firms based on the consistent and compounding effect of revenue.

S Corp - A corporate structure where profits are passed on to the shareholders and taxed on their personal returns.

Scale - Achieving rapid customer adoption (growth) while simultaneously expanding the organization and refining processes to maintain the growth.

Seed Capital - The initial investments made in a startup by someone other than the founder(s).

Series A (or A Round) - A startup's first significant round of funding, which is typically funded by angels.

Series B, C, D, etc. - The subsequent rounds of investments in a startup.

Software Engineer - Individual who designs, develops, tests and maintains software. Unless you want software engineers to increase their fees and hold you in complete contempt for ignorance, don't call them programmers.

Startup - An organization formed to provide a product or service that is being consumed by users or customers.

Startup Idea - A series of hypotheses created with the goal of formulating a startup.

It is very important not to confuse a "Startup" with a "Startup Idea." If you want to lose credibility with successful entrepreneurs, investors etc., tell them you have a startup when you really just have a "startup idea."

Term Sheet - A non-binding agreement between an entrepreneur and investor that ultimately is incorporated into investment agreements (such as an operating agreement).

Trademark - Can be a word, phrase, symbol and/or design that identifies and distinguishes the source of the goods (products) of one party from those of others. Typically, we think of brands, logos, icons and taglines in the startup world when discussing trademarks.

User - Person or organization that consumes a product or service provided by an organization (startup, early stage or mature organization).

User Interface (UI) - Series of screens, pages, buttons and images displayed on a screen (such as a smartphone, laptop or monitor).

User Experience (UX) - The process that a user goes through when interacting with a service (e.g. software) or a product.

Unicorn - A company, within the startup world, valued at more than $1 billion. This is the dream scenario of many entrepreneurs. Just go ahead and buy an island, a jet, a yacht and a couple of new homes. However, many people confuse being a "unicorn" with profitable and sustainable growth. A company could be valued at $1 billion or more but be burning through cash at an unsustainable rate which can lead to rapid devaluation and the need to cut costs, increase revenues or raise more capital.

Valley of Death - The time between initial startup or investment and the time when the startup runs out of cash.

Value Proposition - A statement a startup or organization uses to describe the way it will help its customers.

Venture Capital - Investment made by a group of accredited investors provided by funds or specific firms, typically in exchange for equity.

Venture Capitalists - Individuals who invest in early-stage companies (post-startup phase). Angel investors invest in startups (pre-early-stage companies).

Wantrepreneur - Individual that has a startup idea, but never executes to turn the startup idea into a startup.

About the Author

Dave Gee taught in the MBA program at the University of Wisconsin-Madison. He is currently the co-director of the University of Wisconsin-Whitewater Launch Pad startup accelerator. He mentors startups at gener8tor, a national leading startup accelerator. Dave spent over 20 years working in sales and marketing roles for Fortune 500 companies including Motorola, BellSouth, U.S. Cellular, TDS and Humana.

After leaving the corporate world, he launched his first startup, Sales Sherpas, an advertising agency. Dave then co-founded and was the CEO of Bungee, which provided a software-as-a-service loyalty program. Next, he helped co-found and served as the chief marketing officer for Classmunity, a web-based fundraising management system for school districts. He is currently researching a startup to improve and save the lives of teenagers.

The College Student Startup Guide is his second book. Gee wrote *The Corporate Refugee Startup Guide* to help mid-career professionals launch their startups while balancing their family.

He earned his MBA from Marquette University and his BBA from the University of Wisconsin-Whitewater.

Dave lives with his wife Amy near Lake Geneva, Wisconsin. He enjoys mountain biking, boating and hiking with his family and loyal lab, Caesar.

Learn free startup insights and keep up-to-date with his latest startup on LinkedIn: linkedin.com/in/davidrgee/

CPSIA information can be obtained
at www.ICGtesting.com
Printed in the USA
LVHW031919070120
642794LV00015B/1023/P

9 781687 530752